# PRAYERS

## FOR THE
## WORKING MOM

# PRAYERS

## FOR THE
## WORKING MOM

### 7 SECRETS TO PHENOMENAL SUCCESS

## SABRINA O'MALONE

ACW Press
Eugene, Oregon 97405

**Prayers of the Working Mom: Seven Secrets to Phenomenal Success**
Copyright ©2003 Sabrina O'Malone
All rights reserved

Cover Design by Alpha Advertising
Interior Design by Pine Hill Graphics

Packaged by ACW Press
85334 Lorane Hwy
Eugene, Oregon 97405
www.acwpress.com
The views expressed or implied in this work do not necessarily reflect those of ACW Press. Ultimate design, content, and editorial accuracy of this work is the responsibility of the author(s).

Library of Congress Cataloging-in-Publication Data
*(Provided by Cassidy Cataloguing Services, Inc.)*

O'Malone, Sabrina.

    Prayers for the working mom : 7 secrets to phenomenal success / Sabrina O'Malone. -- Eugene, Ore. : ACW Press, 2003.

    p. ; cm.

    ISBN: 1-932124-20-9

    1. Working mothers--Religious life. 2. Motherhood--Religious aspects. 3. Spiritual life. 4. Prayers. I. Title.

BV4593 .O43 2003
204/.4/082--dc22           0311

**Printed in the United States of America.**

# Dedication

This book is dedicated to those who came before me:

**Stormie Omartian**—Thank you for showing me how to love my God, my husband and children—all at the same time.

**John Maxwell**—Your encouragement has meant the world to me. When I grow up, I want to be like you…only a woman.

**Anna Quindlen**—I'll confess, when you said I was ready to meet the world and make a difference, I had less confidence in myself than you did. Thanks for encouraging me to take the risk of testing my wings.

**Condoleezza Rice**—Until you, I wasn't totally convinced that the glass ceiling could be broken! We're so proud of you. (Ochin-khudershaw!)

**Anne Graham Lotz**—Your message came at exactly the right time.

**Hattie Ridley**—My great-grandmother, the first Negro woman to own and operate an American plantation. We have not forgotten where we came from, and we teach it to our children.

# Contents

# Introduction

"Hey, you look familiar! Don't we know each other?" A young woman with a three-year-old in tow stopped me in the grocery store.

"I was thinking the same thing," I replied. "Don't you work for a pharmaceutical company?"

"Yes, I do," she answered.

"What a beautiful little girl you have." I tousled her daughter's golden locks. "And how have you been?" I asked, redirecting my attention to the mother.

"I'm hanging in there," she responded. "I took the day off to catch up on some paperwork and spend a little extra time with her."

It was already 5:30 P.M. and she was still grocery shopping. She'd be lucky to get dinner ready before 7:00, I thought. Her daughter popped open a bag of organic chips and began to eat them, as if she were reading my mind.

"You do the same kind of work I do…with twice as many kids at home, yet you don't seem frazzled and you look great. How do you do it?" Her eyes held the desperate longing for wisdom that I have seen in the eyes of countless other working mothers.

*Prayers for the Working Mom* was written to answer this heartfelt question. It is my hope and prayer to encourage, inspire and revitalize the busiest people in the world today—the 36 million mothers in America's paid labor force, two out of three of whom are full time!

You've paid your dues...you've worked hard enough. It's high time someone let you in on the secrets to phenomenal success. Welcome to the club. Sit back...relax...and get ready to be amazed.

# Prologue
## A Typical Morning

6:15 A.M.— The buzzing of the alarm clock startles you into the reality that it's time to get going. You press snooze.

6:24 A.M.— Alarm beeps again, but you still have plenty of time. You hit the easiest button, the big wide snooze, of course.

6:33 A.M.— "Beep-Beep" So tired...so sleepy... so justified. You press the snooze button again.

6:42 A.M.— "Beep-beep-beep!" With a sigh, you hit snooze, this time determined to mentally plan out everything you need to do... "Get up, put in contacts, put on beige outfit, find knee-highs in the laundry basket"...as you drift off contentedly to slumber.

6:51 A.M.— "BEEP-BEEP-BEEP!" Now the situation is serious. You crawl out of bed, quietly praying that the kids won't wake up and slow down the process of getting the day started.

7:00 A.M.— By the time you find your other matching sock, you realize you have no time for a shower and that you will have to put on your makeup in the car.

7:15 A.M.— First child wakes up.
Lunches aren't prepared.
You haven't had a quiet time.
Even cereal for breakfast would be a luxury.

7:30 A.M.— One child is dressed and drinking milk
while parked in front of the TV. You begin
to make lunches.

7:45 A.M.— Next child awakes. Frantically, you pick
out what you hope is "all-purpose clothing"
because you haven't a clue of the weather.
With a peep out the window you conclude, "Sweats will be fine."

7:48 A.M.— Child argues. Does not *want* to wear that
outfit. Your temper begins to rise as you
insist.

7:49 A.M.— Child #1 gets bored with TV and requests
a grilled cheese sandwich for breakfast.

It's 8:00! — You run the mental checklist...
+ Any field trips or permission slips
needed today?
+ School fundraisers?
+ Is it show-and-tell day?
+ Library books?

8:03 A.M.— The bus rolls up. Shouting for jackets, caps
and lunchboxes, you commandeer the kids
out the door with a piece of toast and a kiss.

8:05 A.M.— Now you calculate everything you'll need
for work.

8:10 A.M.— While driving to work you realize:

- You haven't taken meat out of the freezer to thaw for dinner.
- You never called your mother back.
- The sink is full of dishes.
- And your husband is down to his last pair of clean underwear.

You pray that God will get you through this day.

8:30 A.M.— After applying makeup haphazardly in the car, you head into work feeling like you've already put in a day's work...before you put in a day's work.

To be honest, this was a pretty smooth morning. The bus wasn't late, none of the kids were sick, the family dog didn't dart out the door and no one needed extra cuddle time. To top it off, the mother made it into work on time...with her makeup on!

Have I gotten your attention? Does this typical morning scenario remind you of someone you know? Chances are that it does because that someone is you! Don't despair; God is waiting to intervene in every difficult morning of your life. Let's invite him in with prayer.

## Prayer

*Lord,*

*I lay all my responsibilities at Your feet. I am now yielding my heart, mind and strength to Your awesome power and glory. I desperately need You.*

Open my eyes, ears, heart and soul so that I'm not too busy to hear You. Teach me to walk, live and be in the center of Your will for my life. Use me as a blessing in the lives of my children, dear Lord.

Forgive me for my past mistakes, which can be better described as sins. I've been impatient, short-tempered, self-righteous and it has made me a difficult woman to love and live with. Lord, starting today, fill me with the fruit of the Spirit: patience, kindness, humility and gentleness.

Make me a woman who is not easily angered; guard me from being rude or selfish. Fill me with the strength to endure all things necessary. Your perfect love never fails. I praise You, and I thank You for saving me.

*Amen.*

## Faith in Action

Circle the 3 words below that cause you the most distress.

| | |
|---|---|
| • Fatigue | • Worry about work |
| • Stress | • Behind in housework |
| • Anxiety about kids | • Lack of finances |
| • Loneliness | • Angry outbursts |
| • Lack of hope | • Discouragement |

Fill in the blanks below with your circled words.

*Lord, I hereby release my* _____,
_____ *and my*
_____ *to You. It is entirely up to*
*You to handle them.*

Circle the 3 corresponding opposites of your list above.

| | |
|---|---|
| • Energy | • Fulfillment |
| • Peace | • Well-run household |
| • Trust and confidence | • Abundance |
| • Companionship | • Words of blessing |
| • Optimism | • Encouragement |

Now fill in the blanks with your newly-circled replacements.

> *Lord, I hereby charge You with the task of filling my*
> *life with* _____, _____
> *and* _____. *With Your help, I will be*
> *like clay being modeled into something beautiful, pur-*
> *poseful and deliberately designed by You, the Master.*
>                                               *Amen.*

(Sign your name below)

X _____ Date _____

# *Secrets*

## to Phenomenal
## Success

# SECRET 1

# Prayer Partners

*"I urge you brothers, by our Lord Jesus*
*Christ and by the love of the Spirit, to join*
*me in my struggle by praying to God for me"*
(Romans 15:30 NIV).

I was three months pregnant with our first child, and was scheduled to have a grapefruit-sized tumor removed from my uterus. The tumor was threatening the pregnancy.

Frankly, I was scared, knowing that an operation on a pregnant woman is very rare because there are risks to both the mother and child. I cried out to God, my husband, friends and relatives. Desperate for a miracle, I turned to my church for prayer. It was then that I saw the church as something more than a building where people go to talk about Jesus.

Several women emerged out of that crisis to become the greatest mentors and prayer partners I know. Most of them are middle-aged, but one lady is 92, another is a teenager. They are all different nationalities, some are married, others are widows, some are single and others are stay-at-home mothers.

These dear women sought me out, called me, sent cards and even brought covered dishes to encourage me in a very tangible way. Each one of them let me know that they were praying for us. Although most of these women were members of our local church, others were believers from different denominations.

I was humbled by the overwhelming love and grace lived out before my eyes.

The morning of the surgery, I prayed like never before for my child. A great big wordless plea of a mother's heart went up before the throne room of God. That's all I could pray before I went under.

*Being a member of the body of Christ avails you to the power of collective prayer.*

I awoke in the recovery room, barely able to utter the question "My baby?"

The operating room nurse looked directly into my eyes, took me by the hand and said, "Sabrina, your baby is fine. Would you like to hear the heartbeat?"

The swishing sound of my baby's heartbeat was like a chorus of angels testifying to God's grace and mercy. I was awed by such amazing grace. My husband and I were not alone in our joy as the entire Presbyterian

Church in New Brunswick, New Jersey rejoiced with us.

I suspect that God would probably have blessed us even if the church had not supported us in prayer. But there is an undeniable value in being able to share the blessings of answered prayer with a group that prays for you and with you.

When my son Daniel was christened, every heart was moved. Many tears of joy were shed that day as everyone remembered their own private and collective prayers for this precious little child.

Being a member of the body of Christ avails you to the power of collective prayer.

The Bible says in Matthew 18:20, "For where two or three come together in my name, there am I with them."

Prayer is the key to opening joy, gratitude, praise and fulfillment to your life, especially when other people support you in prayer. You will have the presence and power of God's Holy Spirit in and throughout your life. This is the Lord's promise to you. He has never broken a promise and He never will.

I can almost hear the questions: "What exactly does that mean, Sabrina?" "How will that make it any easier to get through a day?" I'll share with you another example from my own life.

## Prayer Partners and Marriage

In the months that followed the birth of our second child, I returned to work full-time. At the same time I tried to manage our household and meet the needs of two young children and my husband while being a committed Christian. God had sustained us and blessed us through a very difficult pregnancy. Furthermore, I had two major operations in the months following the birth of my daughter.

Although grateful for my health and the health of my baby, I quickly became overwhelmed. From sunup until well past sundown I was busy. Seriously busy. There was *always* something important that I couldn't quite make the time for.

It wasn't long before I began to actually resent my husband's laid-back demeanor. This was a big change, because his calmness and levelheadedness used to be characteristics I found refreshing. Once the comparisons began, score was kept. Our new favorite word became "I". Our marriage was on a downward spiral and we both knew it.

> With the Lord's help, I asked several women in my church to pray for my marriage—without giving them a whole lot of details.

That's when prayers from others stepped in. I purchased Christian books on marriage and they all instructed "Get your prayer partners to pray for you" (*Winning Your Husband Back* by Gary Smalley and *The Power of a Praying Wife* by Stormie Omartian). I had only one problem.... I didn't have any "prayer partners." As the saying goes, "Desperate times can call for desperate measures."

With the Lord's help, I asked several women in my church to pray for my marriage—without giving them a whole lot of details.

Each one of them said they would be happy to do it. Then I began to pray for my husband. We instituted a weekly date night and attended a "Family Life Today" marriage conference, all while being lifted up in prayer.

The changes between us were nothing less than dramatic. Our marriage had new life within the first few days. Over the next few months, things continued to improve. I am happy to report that now we are even more in love and more of a team than when we first married. I attribute these changes to God's grace and the impact of prayer.

## For Women Only

Asking someone else to pray for your particular situation can be intimidating. Thus, it's important that you carefully and prayerfully select your prayer partners based on their character. I cannot emphasize enough selecting *only* women as intimate prayer partners, mainly because the Bible encourages women of all ages to maintain relationships with one another (see Titus).

Just imagine all the potential areas of temptation involved in sharing your innermost thoughts, challenges and feelings with someone of the opposite sex. Unless this man is your husband, reaching this degree of emotional intimacy is a red flag signaling danger! Most affairs begin with some kind of "connection." Even if you would never entertain the thought, a male "good friend" might. And thoughts like that can—and will—take away from the original purpose, which is prayer for you about a specific challenge or struggle.

Establishing faith-based relationships with women who are not given to gossip and who love the Lord will enable you to move mountains.

Proverbs 31:25 describes a godly woman like this: "She is clothed with strength and dignity; she can laugh at the days to come. She speaks with wisdom and faithful instruction is on her tongue." We find a similar passage in Titus 2:3: "Likewise teach the older women to be reverent in the way they live, not to be slanderers or addicted to much wine, but to teach what is good."

> *Establishing faith-based relationships with women who are not given to gossip and who love the Lord will enable you to move mountains.*

Can you think of any women who are strong, dignified and laugh a lot? Can you think of an older woman who is reverent, a woman whom you've never heard say a bad thing about anyone? If so, she would probably be honored to hear you tell her that she reminds you of the "Proverbs 31" woman. And this is the type of woman you could trust to commit any situation of yours to prayer.

If you are a working mother who doesn't know any women like this within your circle of acquaintances, do not worry. Fortunately, in God's loving-kindness, He has made a provision for you. It is called the church. Ask your pastor to recommend some women who would fit the bill.

## Did She Say the Church?

Yes, I did. However, I cannot ignore the sincerity and devotion I've seen in the lives of many of my non-churchgoing friends. This is why this book has been written to benefit *all* working moms by using a Bible-based Judeo-Christian perspective.

I pray that God will use me to reflect His love, His grace and His compassion. If there have been poor examples of Christianity that have tainted your opinion of Christians as a whole, I pray that getting to know me better will reflect positively on Jesus Christ, and his church.

## Prayer Partners and Children

The stories in this book are true. They are about regular, normal women who have experienced God's miraculous grace through the power of prayer, and who have been kind enough to give me permission to share God's miracles in their lives. I pray that you will be as encouraged and uplifted by the testimonies of Sherri and Sandy as I have been.

The story of Sherri beautifully illustrates how collective prayer and having prayer partners and mentors can enrich the life of a working mother. She became a believer at the age of eighteen, and, as is the case with most eighteen-year-old women, she anxiously looked forward to marriage in her future. Thirteen years later, the Lord sent her Robert, a godly man whom she adored and married within a year.

Sherri is an ebullient, joyful woman who positively glows with the love of the Lord. To know her is to recognize that she has a valuable spiritual gift in that she is extremely easy to like. A few years into Sherri and Robert's marriage, there were still no children. If you or any of your friends have ever struggled with infertility, then you know how this can steal your joyful countenance.

After praying for over a year on their own, Sherri and Robert enlisted the prayer support of their church. Sherri already had some Christian women in her life that she considered friends, but when she asked them to pray with her about such a personal struggle, the depth of those relationships increased. Her Christian friends became her prayer warriors and her prayer warriors became mentors.

> *Mentors are absolutely vital for a working mother.*

Mentors are absolutely vital for a working mother.

A mentoring relationship can be described like this: Picture yourself as a small, tired child. (So far, this should be easy for any working mother.) Now, envision yourself climbing into the lap of a loving mother. Imagine yourself being rocked and comforted while she gently strokes your hair.

After a meaningful conversation with a mentor, you will feel as secure as this child. Working mothers desperately need this relationship of receiving wisdom, love and nurturing. It is available to you if you'll begin by asking a few trustworthy women to pray for you. Then ask the Lord to develop these relationships into mentorships.

Sherri did, and she has been richly blessed because of it. One January morning, Sherri received something that very few of us are privileged to receive. While praying to the Lord in her car about her husband's health, she heard the voice of the Lord saying audibly, "I have heard your prayers and will give you the desires of your heart. Your husband's diabetes will be under control and I will bless you with children." This encouraged her soul, as you can imagine.

After many years of waiting and trying, Sherri gave birth to a son named Jacob on Father's Day. (Robert said that this gift surely topped the leaf blower Sherri bought him the year before.)

The prayers of the righteous avail much!

## Prayer Partners and Health

The second woman, Sandy, is a person who knows all too well what the above verse means. She has heard the three words that no one wants to hear from their doctor: "You have cancer."

Sandy is the mother of two daughters and was working full time as a medical practice administrator when she received the diagnosis. After sharing the news with her family, one of her daughters asked, "When are you going to die from this, Mom?"

That heartfelt, naïve question ignited the sparks of Sandy's faith. Possessing the peace that passes understanding in regard to her cancer, she made a vow that this wouldn't take her. Although Sandy wasn't particularly religious, she scheduled a prayer circle meeting at her home the night before her operation.

As a matter of course, she sent out an internal e-mail at her job telling her co-workers of her upcoming surgery. She included in the e-mail that her family would be together at 6 P.M. on that particular night before her surgery and they welcomed any well wishes, thoughts and prayers.

Unbeknown to Sandy, one of her co-workers forwarded the e-mail to her mother, who sent it on to a local church. Another co-worker forwarded the e-mail to her sister in Germany. Sandy's prayer request quickly traveled all over the world.

> *All those who were present burst into tears! This manifestation of the Holy Spirit moved even the hardest of hearts.*

The night of the prayer circle arrived and a small group of Sandy's relatives assembled in her home. Not all of them were believers, including her father, yet when they began to pray a visible white light and an overwhelming sense of peace came down and surrounded the circle.

All those who were present burst into tears! This manifestation of the Holy Spirit moved even the hardest of hearts.

We serve an awesome God of love, peace and rest.

And He still works miracles because when Sandy went in for her operation the next morning, there was no cancer to be found. And it hasn't returned in three years!

Expressions such as "Rejoice, be glad, praise and give thanks" hardly seem adequate when God performs a miracle. Even if you have yet to experience or recognize God's miraculous handiwork in your own life, pray and praise Him with me right now.

## Prayer

Lord,

Thank You, Lord, for Your promise to supply all of my needs. Thank You for the countless times You've saved me and blessed me, especially those times when I never knew You were there.

The Bible says that You are always with me; You'll never leave me or forsake me. This is the kind of love I've longed for my entire life. With all power and strength in your hands, You know me completely and love me still. You provide for me and protect me. You even gave Your life to save mine.

Help me to know that in Your strength I can do all things. Having prayer partners and mentors sounds wonderful. As I lay my needs before You, I pray that you would strengthen me, and make me bold enough to ask my sisters in the Lord to pray for my family and for me.

Put the right godly women in my life, Lord. Guard my heart, thoughts and actions from things that displease You. Keep me from evil. I pray without ceasing that You would bless my family abundantly and mold us into exactly what You would have us to be. Use me, as an instrument of Your divine will.

Amen.

## Faith in Action

List the names of several women you can ask to pray for you.

_____

_____

_____

_____

_____

Write down the specific needs you want them to pray about.

_____

_____

_____

_____

Pray for these women right now, asking God to bless them, their families and their walk with God.

_____

_____

_____

_____

SECRET

2

# Eliminate the Extraneous

*"Everything is permissible—but not everything is beneficial. Everything is permissible—but not everything is constructive"* (1 Corinthians 10:23 NIV).

As a working mother, you've probably already noticed that you spend a great deal of time just being pressed for time. Your time is valuable to your God, your family, your employer and to you—which is why you must consciously decide what things are beneficial and constructive, thereby making them worth your investment of time.

If you already feel overwhelmed, then it's time to take stock of your commitments and examine how you spend your time off the clock. It may be possible that you don't need to be such an integral member of all the worthy causes you are currently committed to—at least at this stage in your life. The Bible tells us that the Lord's yoke is easy and His burden is light.

## Your Life, Your Garden

Our first story is an analogy shared with me by Enid, a busy mother of five children.

A young woman decided to take up the hobby of gardening. She purchased everything she needed, including a how-to manual about the subject and she set out with vigor to create her garden.

She selected a location with the right amount of sunlight and shade, the right topsoil and even meticulously measured the depth, width and spacing required. Soon the little seedlings appeared. She was overjoyed! She could already envision the fruit that would someday be hers.

She continued to read the manual and, to her dismay, the book instructed her to pull out every other seedling! She read it twice to be certain. "Did this apply to her particular garden?" she questioned. She went out and examined her creation.

Each precious plant was growing beautifully and, to her eye, it seemed obvious they had plenty of space and room to continue to do so. There was nothing wrong with any of them.

"Perhaps," she thought, "the instructions apply to *other* gardeners who have something else growing. Mine are doing quite well, and I've already promised to give the fruit to people who really need it. I simply couldn't cut this crop in half!" She did not have the heart to pull any of them up and they all continued to grow...for a while.

Any experienced gardener can tell you the folly of this woman's decision. Underneath the ground, the roots told a different story. Eventually, the roots became entangled and tight. No plant could reach its full potential under those conditions and, ultimately, none of her plants bore any fruit.

There is nothing inherently wrong with joining the PTA, being a scout leader, belonging to an auxiliary club or serving on the school board.

Nor is there anything wrong with a few extra-curricular activities for your children—be it soccer, football, ballet lessons, karate, piano lessons or cheerleading. These are all good things.

The problem arises when there are so many activities that the family struggles to keep up with the hectic schedule. The carpooling and errands associated with these extra-curricular pursuits may not be where the Lord would have your family expend its time and energy.

> *It can be hard to let go of something good, especially when it's just to make room for "free time."*

It can be hard to let go of something good, especially when it's just to make room for "free time."

The temporary anguish associated with cutting back, however, is worth the long-term joy of experiencing a peaceful, less hectic family life. Pray about which of your own painstakingly planted "seedlings" need to be pulled out. I am already praying with you.

## Feeding without Getting Fed

Overcommitting yourself to the noble calling of church work may not even be God's will for you right now.

The following story is the perfect illustration of the temptation we feel to go "all out" in the name of serving God. Can you imagine the joyous anticipation you would feel if a group of fifteen of the most recognizable leaders in Christianity decided to have dinner and fellowship at your home?

One woman doesn't have to imagine, because it happened to her! Martha, blessed with the spiritual gift of hospitality, had a legitimate reason to put her best foot forward.

She had to cook enough food for fifteen people, create a place for them to sit and apply the finishing touches to make this a memorable experience. She wisely called her sister for help as their hometown was out of the way of caterers and large supermarket chains. Everyone arrived together. What joy she felt to see her home so used by the Lord!

"What can I get you to drink?" she asked.

"Just water, thank you. I'm parched."

"Me, too."

"That goes double for me!"

"I'll have a glass of wine, the red."

"Sounds good!"

"I'll take some of your white wine."

"I'll have a glass of that, too."

"How about ale?"

"Yeah, ale for me, too!"

Everyone seemed to answer simultaneously. She was more grateful than ever that she had her sister there to help.

"I'll get those drinks while you all sit down at the table and enjoy some fresh baked bread and appetizers."

After Martha poured the drinks, she realized her work was just beginning; she still had to serve the main course. That's when she noticed her sister, just sitting there with the guests, listening with complete fascination to what was undoubtedly a great story.

Maybe it was nerves or stress, but the sight made Martha mad—so mad that she chose to bring this situation before the Lord immediately.

"Lord, don't you care that my sister has left me do the work by myself? Tell her to help me!" she complained.

Frankly, I would have done the same thing. But she received an answer that was not what she expected. "Martha, Martha," the Lord answered, "you are worried and upset about many things, but only one thing is needed. Mary has chosen what is better, and it will not be taken away from her" (Luke 10:38-42).

> Here's some food for thought: The very same Jesus Martha worked so hard to feed is the Man who fed 5,000 people with one little boy's lunch...

You guessed it, this story comes from the Holy Bible, and it's just as relevant today as it was when Jesus spoke those words to Martha herself. The account of Mary and Martha serves to remind us that we're not expected to work so hard to serve God that we miss the opportunity to enjoy Him and listen to Him!

Here's some food for thought: The very same Jesus Martha worked so hard to feed is the Man who fed 5,000 people with one little boy's lunch. It was Jesus who turned water into fine wine at a wedding celebration.

Did He really need Martha to knock herself out to get everyone fed? Does He really need you to serve on every committee that asks you?

My mother says, "When God calls you to do something, He'll make a way for it to be done." You are obviously called to be a mother and, with God's help, He'll make a way for you to have the time you need to do that mothering.

If you feel pressed for time, minimizing or eliminating your non-essential involvements will free you to take care of higher priority activities. Just being more relaxed and available to your family may be the higher priority the Lord has for you now. Remember, if it is getting more and more difficult for you to keep up with the pace of your lifestyle and commitments, it may God's way of telling you to re-prioritize.

## The Telephone

Yvette is a busy mother of three children. She holds a part-time job in retail sales and happens to be one of the most organized women I know. She is a natural mentor, and many people are drawn to her.

Yvette's phone used to ring constantly with people needing advice, wanting to vent (also known as gossip) or, occasionally, some callers would ask for prayer. Eventually, her "ministry" began to take its toll on her family.

She found herself increasingly absorbed trying to handle other people's problems and situations. Her family frequently had to wait while she handled an urgent phone call from one of her friends. It wasn't long before her own relationship with her family began to suffer.

"Honey, would you mind finishing dinner? I just got a call that really needs my attention."

"Kids, I'm on the phone! Go ask your father!"

It is easy to see that too much of this would drain any family. Fortunately, Yvette discovered a way to minimize distractions at home—without having to engage in emotionally draining confrontations with her callers.

A new day dawned when her answering machine "broke." Yvette discovered that the machine (which she loved before the kids were born) no longer served as a convenience. In fact, the answering machine added things to her already extensive to-do list. She prayerfully decided to not to replace it; however, she secretly obtained a caller ID! Now she selects the times and the people with whom she will speak—and she makes those selections without offending anyone.

> *Deliberately spend more time interacting with the people who build you up, and more time praying to God for the people who drain you.*

Yvette's callers are typically divided into two categories: edifying relationships (prayer partners and mentors) and ministry opportunities (people to pray for or witness to). You need to prayerfully make a distinction between people who drain you and people who build you up.

Deliberately spend more time interacting with the people who build you up, and more time praying to God for the people who drain you.

Even if you don't utilize Yvette's "broken answering machine" strategy, you can be in a position to consciously decide the best use of your time. Answering machines, call waiting, pagers and cell phones can take away your choice of how to spend your time. The broken answering machine may be your ticket to more time with your family, particularly if you can't find the time to return every message left.

If after a hard day's work, you frequently find yourself talking on the phone, while stirring a pot on the stove and simultaneously shushing the kids, consider this: By dividing your time this way, you are not operating at optimum efficiency.

> There is a God—
> and He isn't you!

For starters, you can't give your caller your undivided attention. Furthermore, this is not meaningful interaction between you and your children. And the clincher: You run the risk of making a mess of your dinner. (Have you ever seasoned food twice because you were distracted? I certainly have.)

If you can relate a little to well too Yvette's story of the constantly ringing phone, then you have plenty of company. Phone time is one of the most popular non-essential time expenditures.

Also, if you are under the impression that you are obligated to listen, offer advice and let anyone with problems vent to you at any time, let me encourage you with this.

There is a God—and He isn't you!

The fact that you are always available may be the very thing keeping someone from a deeper walk with the

Lord. It is possible to be more comfortable turning to a fallible, fallen human being than to God. As much as any person loves another, only God can truly save.

In God's loving providence, there are professional telephone ministries equipped to handle emotional and spiritual crises. While there is no substitute for prayer, spending time reading the Bible or having a nice chat with a mentor, remember that an ongo-

> *The fact that you spend time away from your kids while you work makes it even more vital that you be mentally at home—when you're at home.*

ing crisis may be beyond your ability or your mentor's. For more tangible help, (800) NEW-LIFE and (888) NEED-HIM have someone available twenty-four hours a day.

Let these thoughts give you strength as you begin to direct your friends and your life towards the Lord.

You are not living to please others. (It's futile.)

You are not living to please yourself. (It's selfish.)

You are living to please God, and He loves you with an everlasting love. Furthermore, He's entrusted you with children, an indescribable gift and blessing.

The fact that you spend time away from your kids while you work makes it even more vital that you be mentally at home—when you're at home.

All children have a legitimate need for their mother's time and attention.

## The Television

Delia is a nurse in a high-stress neonatal intensive care unit of a busy hospital. She is also the mother of three children under the age of five. Her story reveals how she increased the amount of quality interaction time with her family by reducing the use of television.

Delia and Roger started out like any other couple. Before they had children, they had cable TV and watched movies and football games on their television set. Each day they watched the news. While Delia was pregnant with their first child, she became increasingly sensitive to the violence on television, and made a decision to start watching only wholesome programming.

After the birth of their child, Delia actually felt relieved when the baby was old enough to pay attention to the TV set. Thanks to the "purple dinosaur," she was *almost* able to keep up with her cooking, cleaning and bill paying. But it didn't sit right with her. She remembered that she had vowed (in her youthful pre-baby exuberance) never to use the television as an electronic babysitter…but somehow it had happened. Delia cut back her hours at work, but still yearned for more time with Roger and the baby. That's when she realized she could use the time spent watching television to interact with Roger and their toddler.

Just as she began to implement the new plan, she was pregnant again and exhausted. Roger had started a new job and they had moved to a new house. The temptation to go back to the videos was tremendous. Her in-laws, friends (including me) and acquaintances all questioned the viability of having a no-TV family. What would she do when she really needed the kids to be still and quiet for an hour? Isn't it meaningful interaction to watch a wholesome show on television if you do it together as a family?

Delia's home life tells a fascinating story. When she needs quiet, she pulls out special project toys (clay or markers or some other kind of craft). The kids celebrate these coveted "special" toys. Every night her toddlers "help" her make dinner. It keeps them busy, quiet and nearby, even if they're not much help. Delia's children create all sorts of wonderful gifts, and they are quietly absorbed in their activities when she needs them to be.

This sounds a whole lot more enriching than my own plan for quiet. "Pop in a video" was my motto for years! Delia, however, is a working mother who spends almost all of her off-the-clock time finding ways to integrate home activities with quality family time. Getting out of the TV habit played a vital role in her ability to develop such a strong family relationship.

Even busy families seem to find the time to tie up two or more hours a day watching television. Allow me to share with you (the working mother) several reasons to consider putting your family on a low television diet.

The first reason is money. In the Northeastern United States, cable television can be expensive, often more than $60 per month. If a family utilizes pay-per-view, that amount can quickly escalate. There is also the cost of having your family influenced by commercials to purchase greater quantities of things that aren't really necessary. Fiscally, cable television cannot be considered economical entertainment.

Second, can "educational" or "wholesome" programs really compare with sitting down together to read a book or having a discussion with one another? You are face to face during conversation; you exchange ideas, thoughts

41

and feelings. When you read a story, you can stop and start; it will still be there. There is eye contact between the pages, and the ability to fully answer questions without missing anything simply because the story waits for you and goes at your pace. Television does not.

It is not easy to maintain a conversation while watching TV. Some would argue that it is actually rude to try, and that it would be more polite to talk later…but as a busy working mother, you know all too well that there is no later. If you have only a few hours between when you get home and your kids go to bed, how reasonable is it to expect anything to happen later?

*It doesn't make sense to let anything other than God have so much priority in your family.*

It doesn't make sense to let anything other than God have so much priority in your family.

It is not my intention to suggest that every working mother eliminate the television set from her home. Watching TV is not always bad. I recognize the benefits that can be derived from obtaining information and entertainment from both a visual and auditory medium. The more senses involved, the more likely a message will register, which can be a great tool for learning. Prayerfully consider, however, whether or not the television has become a stumbling block in your family's life. If your children prefer to spend time in their rooms watching their own favorite shows on their own private sets, rather than spending time together as a family, think about ways to draw them away from the sets and towards the family.

## Starting the Low-TV Diet

So far, this is easier said than done. How can you possibly put your own family on a low-television diet? The way to gain family cooperation is astonishingly simple. To start with, convince their father...and use economics. As I mentioned before, in my area cable television costs about $60 per month. $60 per month times 12 months = $720 per year! If Dad is fiscally minded, or has a frugal/thrifty disposition, he may be convinced as soon as you mention a way to save $720 every year!

If Dad watches a lot of TV himself, and it's usually sports, then this tip is for you. Find out the price of season tickets to his favorite local sports team. If they cost less than you're paying per year for cable, "Voila!" Suggest that he see the games in person!

If you'll promise to baby-sit without complaint when he wants to go to a game, 99 percent of the sports fans in the world would support getting rid of cable and satellite TV. Another benefit for you is that no sport is played all year long, and they all have games away from home and weather cancellations. Consequently, during the entire "off-season," the whole family can enjoy life with fewer TV distractions.

> *With prayer and God's grace, you may actually net out more hours of real family time by resorting to the season-ticket strategy.*

With prayer and God's grace, you may actually net out more hours of real family time by resorting to the season-ticket strategy.

How will you get the kids to accept this without emotional turmoil? Start by explaining and describing the benefits they will receive when they minimize the use of television for entertainment. Paint a verbal picture for them of how they will experience more of the things that they already enjoy about family life.

> *You won't disappoint your kids if you do your homework.*

This is important. There is an age-old concept called "WIIFM" which answers the unspoken question in everyone's heart: "What's in it for me?" There is a difference between telling someone, "This is for your own good," versus describing all the specific good that will occur for them.

You won't disappoint your kids if you do your homework.

For example, if your ten-year-old loves to play chess, by all means describe what it will be like to have time to play nightly chess games. If your preteen likes baking, describe the confections that she will have the time to create and how her treats will marvel the family. Describe the reception she'll receive at school when she comes in with samples!

There are myriad benefits that can motivate children of all ages. You can probably think of other ideas to motivate your children. Find a way to tie them in with compliance to the new family policy.

If you aren't sure what they would enjoy, ask the question, "Other than watching TV or playing video games, what do you like to do at home the most?" When you ask this question *before* you unveil the low television diet, their answers will provide the keys to motivating each particular child, and will also give you some insight into their world.

As a word to the wise, decide in advance a reasonable amount of television time for the whole family. Dividing up time for each family member's television show preferences creates the possibility of dividing up your family's interaction time.

Consider instituting rewards for compliance (especially compliance without complaints). An extra bedtime story for the little ones, a board game with older ones or even special "coffee break with Mom" times for adolescents may go a long way towards encouraging the family to make the adjustment.

> *Trust your instincts. You know what will best motivate your child.*

Trust your instincts. You know what will best motivate your child.

Even if your children vehemently protest initially (and some of them will), you can rest assured that cutting back on civic commitments, telephone time and television are the right things to do. Your family will, in fact, become acclimated to a simplified lifestyle and your family dynamics will be infinitely richer because of it.

## Prayer

Lord,

I recognize that I am overcommitted. This burden is not easy nor is it light. Everything I participate in is good, but the sum of so many good things is evidently too heavy for me to carry.

I ask that You would give me vision to see what I should eliminate, give me the courage to let it go, then bless me with peace and strength when I make the changes.

Soften the hearts of my family, friends, church and civic committees. Let them accept these changes with grace. Put the desire to take charge of the good things that I relinquish into the heart of someone else.

I'm excited at the prospect of increasing the quality of time I spend with my family, Lord. I praise You for blessing me with Your love and acceptance. I'm grateful that Your favor is a gift, not dependent on my activities or my human goodness.

Never let me forget that when I try to earn Your blessings with my "good" activities, it becomes wages…and I already work enough. Remind me that You've given me a free will and the promise of peace and joy.

I can't please everyone, and trying to do so has run me ragged. Help me to concentrate on pleasing You alone.

*Amen.*

Faith in Action

List all the extraneous activities in your life.

_____

_____

_____

_____

_____

Which of these would have to be eliminated to increase the number of meals your family can share together every week?

_____

_____

_____

_____

What pulls your family's at-home time apart the most—the TV, computer or phone? Set a limit now on how much time your family will spend on these things.

_____

_____

_____

_____

# Delegation

*"You and these people who come to you will only wear yourselves out. The work is too heavy for you; you cannot handle it alone"* (Exodus 18:18 NIV).

Delegate? I don't have time to delegate!"
"I don't have anyone to delegate to!"
"They wouldn't do it right."

"I'd have to fight to get them to do it, then I'd have to inspect it once it's done. It's easier to just do it myself."

I hear you. I've been there myself. But there's a secret you've probably never been privy to. It goes beyond wishing someone else would lend a hand and complaining if they don't. It's time for action, real solutions that make delegation actually happen.

You have taken the first step in deciding to pray with prayer partners. And you know the second secret and have decided to eliminate extraneous activities.

Congratulations, this is a great start. What's now left in your life cannot be eliminated and must be done.

But does it really *have* to be done by *you?*

If the Scripture verse above resonates deep within you, or if it seems God is specifically talking about *your* life, then this chapter is for you. You simply can't do it all by yourself and fortunately, God does not expect you to.

There are benefits to everyone (including you) when you delegate your workload appropriately. It's always tough to delegate, but for a busy working mom, it can seem almost impossible.

To use an analogy, being a working mom is very much like juggling. Learning to juggle takes practice, and it's especially stressful if the items you juggle are valuable and fragile.

It's hard to juggle three things, harder still to juggle four. Difficulty and stress increase with each addition. Ultimately, even the best jugglers will drop the ball. This is precisely what any working mom wishes to avoid while trying to keep up with schedules, work demands and running a household.

When so many balls are juggling in the air, trying to stop so you can reduce the number increases the risk that something will fall by the wayside. This is the inherent risk in deciding whether and how to delegate. Believe me, I know you can't afford to let anything drop.

However, you should be aware of the flip side to managing everything yourself. Sooner or later, your aching back will give out, then you'll be unable to do anything for weeks.

The tension from maintaining this high-stress lifestyle can show up as frequent headaches, or maybe you'll end up eating Rolaids like candy in an attempt to settle your constantly churning stomach. Stress often leads to anxiety and, in the worst case scenario, panic attacks. Take it from me, one way or another, your body and mind will not allow you to keep up with more than you can bear.

> *Every working mom can successfully delegate some of her responsibilities.*

Fortunately, there is hope... even for the toughest case scenario of single working mom with young children and limited finances.

Every working mom can successfully delegate some of her responsibilities.

Diane, a former working mom with four girls, shared an innovative solution with me. She vividly remembered from her days of working outside the home that the most difficult part of the day was getting dinner ready. She suspected other working moms might have the same problem so she called a few of her friends and asked if they would like her to make extra portions of what she planned to cook for dinner.

Diane would put an entire meal in disposable containers and leave it at the doorstep of her working friend's house in exchange for a portion of their grocery/takeout budget. Because Diane buys in bulk now, her food cost is lower and she can pocket the extra cash.

Remember, it's not extra work for Diane, because it's what she cooked for her family anyway. Now the working mom gets to come home to an inexpensive, hot, home-cooked meal!

> *Just imagine what it would be like to come home after a hard day's work to be greeted by the smell of already made dinner! Now that's a blessing.*

If any of your friends are stay-at-home moms, ask if they would be willing to give this a try one or two days a week.

Just imagine what it would be like to come home after a hard day's work to be greeted by the smell of already made dinner! Now that's a blessing.

## The Man Around the House

The question always arises concerning household workload and what "he" ought to do versus what "she" does. I'll share with you three bits of advice I received from my mother on my wedding day:

"First, lower your expectations, Sabrina."

"Second, laugh at his jokes."

"Third, remember that a marriage requires 100 percent flexibility. Ninety percent of that flexing is going to come from the wife."

That last bit of advice sounded downright silly and old-fashioned to me. I thought to myself, "Maybe in your generation, Mom, but we're going to have a 50-50 marriage."

My husband (Dan) later explained to me why he thinks my mom was right. What causes more sadness and heartbreak than unmet expectations? Generally speaking, it is more pleasant to have your expectations exceeded than fallen short of.

Next, when you laugh at someone's jokes it is the most sincere form of applause and opens the door to a great deal of joy. As the Bible says, "Laughter is good medicine."

Lastly, it is easy to recognize when you accommodate, or flex, for your spouse. It's never as clear when someone else is flexing for you. Even if a 50-50 partnership were possible in marriage, you would *always* be more aware of your effort than his.

*Always.*

My suggestion is that you be very careful and prayerful about delegating to your husband. The temptation to go on the "must-be-nice-to-be-you" bandwagon is nearly impossible to resist, and that bandwagon is ultimately counterproductive. Believe me, I've tried it.

You probably work as hard as he does. You may even do more than the majority of women you know. But expecting him to be an assistant homemaker will almost certainly lead to disappointment.

Try to remember, most men today contribute more around the house than their father did. And if you keep a running tally of your tasks versus his, it will not lead to a harmonious family life.

It just won't.

The Bible refers to this as "keeping a record of wrongs" (1 Corinthians 13:5).

You have a choice: Is it more important to prove yourself to be "right" or to have harmony in the home?

> *When you need affirmation, appreciation and understanding for all that you do and you can't get it from your husband, go to the Lord!*

When you need affirmation, appreciation and understanding for all that you do and you can't get it from your husband, go to the Lord!

Look in your concordance for passages about God's love for you and how precious you are to Him and read them. Then go to your prayer partners and mentors for a little encouragement. It will be a lot easier to let go of your record of wrongs when you are filled with God's love.

Practically speaking, what's an overstressed overburdened working mom to do? I'll tell you what I did. First, I prayed about my situation...frequently. Next, I resolved to pay closer attention to my husband's strengths and look for ways he could contribute towards managing our family that would naturally suit his demeanor.

I recognized that my husband is a playful guy, and he loves to spend time horsing around with the kids. Whenever he gave the kids a bath, they had a great time and got clean, but the watery soapy mess they left behind was simply something else for me to clean up (or nag about). My own style of "Wet down, soap up, rinse off!" was efficient, quick and neat, but certainly not fun.

"Lord, show me how we can both use our strengths," I prayed. He was quick to show me the way. I am naturally in a hurry. After dinner, I usher the kids through their routine: military style baths, putting on pajamas, brushing teeth until Daddy swoops in like a breath of fresh air.

My husband now puts the kids to bed at night. They play, read, recount their day and say bedtime prayers with him. I take my exit and am free to do whatever needs to be done, or just retire early.

There are times when the whole ordeal takes them two full hours after I leave. But, as a student of my husband, I observed that long, drawn-out processes don't upset him like they do me. This is a great method to utilize our respective strengths to the benefit of our family.

I also perceived that he takes a lot of pride in finding bargains at the grocery store. On the occasions when he has gone shopping alone, he proudly displays the receipts showing the percentage he saved using his shoppers card or buying in bulk.

So I should just let him take over the task of grocery shopping, right? But is it really that simple? No, because I came up against the hurdle most of us encounter with delegating important tasks. Sometimes we have differing definitions of what is an important task is.

Furthermore, I used the typical Mommy-style grocery shopping method of "walking-down-the-aisles-and-spotting-what-we-need-as-I-go-along." I certainly couldn't expect Dan to do that. When I tried to write out a list for him, I found myself mentally exhausted trying to remember everything, and it took almost as much time to make the list as to do the shopping myself!

It seemed like the "pros" of delegating grocery shopping equaled the "cons." These quandaries led to the creation of the Working Mom Grocery checklist (see page 133). It's a fast, thorough, one-page list that can even be faxed. Simply put a checkmark next to what you need, print it out, and in less than three minutes, you have a foolproof list.

(There is also a free, easy-to-print form on our website: <www.workingmom.com>)

## Get Rid of the Guilt

Perhaps you are questioning whether it would be better for the kids if you didn't work at all. Or maybe you're feeling guilty about the choices you've made in life which have put you in your current situation and you're trying to "make it up" to the kids with fewer at-home requirements. If so, please stop it.

> *Please take this to heart…it is not a sin to work while you have children. It may even be a part of God's plan for you and your family.*

Some working moms feel that because they are away from their kids so many hours during the day, they don't want their precious time together to be spent fighting about chores. Consequently, very little is expected of the children as far as pitching in around the house.

This is an example of what the Bible calls "false guilt," and it does not come from God. True guilt, or conviction about a wrongdoing, can be an important motivator if it prompts making a beneficial change. But it is *always* false guilt if no sin has been committed.

Please take this to heart...it is not a sin to work while you have children. It may even be a part of God's plan for you and your family.

This can be hard to accept. When you so passionately love your children and so strongly want what is best for them, it's difficult to imagine that being apart could be anything more than second best. I've been there, and I empathize completely.

One of my mentors encouraged me with the following advice: "You've got to remember that you are raising future adults, and childhood is when they learn responsibility. When you have 'your reasons' for not setting and enforcing realistic expectations, the kids will grow up to be poorly equipped to meet their own family expectations in the future. It would be a disservice to their future spouse and children."

These guilty feelings that cause you to set lax standards for behavior and household work requirements are not your friend. They don't ultimately help your children, so just let them go. If this is difficult for you, you will need to ask your prayer partners and mentors to support you in your struggle.

A word to the wise: Anyone who has ever belittled you for working, or patronized you with "I don't know how you do it, I'm just so glad I can stay home with my kids," would not be the person to go to when you are already struggling with this kind of false guilt.

Put simply, all kids (even the kids of working moms) should be required to do regular unpaid work around the

> At the risk of stating the obvious, every child can pitch in. Even a two-year-old can be taught to put away toys.

house. It's for their own good…it's also for your own good!

At the risk of stating the obvious, every child can pitch in. Even a two-year-old can be taught to put away toys.

Three and four year olds can be taught to fold washcloths and dishtowels. Once they have learned their colors, they can easily sort laundry into dark colors, light colors and whites.

As kids get older, they have the ability to handle more work around the house. The first step in assigning household work is to know what they are capable of. I have enclosed a chart in the appendix section that provides general guidelines of age appropriate housework.

This leads us to the recurring question, "How on earth will I get them to do it?" There are multiple answers to this dilemma. A great deal of your success in this endeavor will depend on the relationship you have established with your child, the child's overall demeanor and yours.

I would like to make a suggestion that should benefit every situation…remember to answer the WIIFM question (What's In It For Me?).

When my brother and I were young, the WIIFM was usually, "You will avoid a spanking, lecture, and/or being grounded if you comply." For my brother, that was usually enough to elicit obedience. For me, those methods induced a sense of trepidation…as I consciously chose to disobey, despite the warning.

There are no quick and easy one-size-fits-all formulas to getting every child to do what they're told. If you have ever been the mother of a two year old, you know how right I am. However, a consequence coupled with an enticement substantially increases the likelihood of compliance in almost every managerial situation (including motherhood).

Going back to my own situation, when I was growing up, my parents discovered that they could gain remarkable results from their headstrong daughter if they used the enticement of car privileges.

"Sabrina, I'll let you take my car out to get some ice cream if you finish cleaning up the kitchen before dark." That really motivated me.

But my parents used more than just enticements. One of their most widely used consequences hit me where I felt it the most...

"If this room is not cleaned up by the time I get home from work, I'm unplugging your telephone, and you won't get it back until I'm ready for you to have it!" For a very social child, this served as the hammer of punishments, the one I sought to avoid with all of my being.

> Each child is different. Study your child carefully and it will be clear how to best motivate, as well as how to administer the most effective consequences.

Using these same tactics on my brother, however, were completely ineffective. His demeanor is different from mine, and he fairly shrugged at gaining car privileges or the loss of his telephone. What he couldn't do without were his video games; thus, the loss of these served as the hammer of all consequences for him. He could be motivated by the promise of getting new basketball cards.

Each child is different. Study your child carefully and it will be clear how to best motivate, as well as how to administer the most effective consequences.

## What If They Get Mad at Me for This?

Some mothers describe their still-at-home children as their best friends. On the surface, this sounds idyllic, but these mothers are at a disadvantage in disciplinary situations. Every time discipline or correction is called for, she runs the risk of losing her best friend. This creates a situation that a child is not mature enough to handle.

For a best friend, look to your prayer partners and mentors. This is just another reason why establishing Prayer Partners was the first secret to phenomenal success. You will find a frequent need for them.

## Professional Help

Even with the entire family pitching in around the house, if finances allow for it, bringing in an occasional cleaning service can free up a lot of time and energy. I highly recommend it. Be sure to ask your acquaintances if they know of someone who's trustworthy and thorough. If you have to resort to the phone book or a newspaper advertisement, be sure to check the references.

I have a friend who lived far from family when she had her first child. She returned to work full time and refused to hire a housekeeper, even though they had enough money. She said every time she brought someone in, they didn't do as good a job as she could do for herself. She figured, why pay someone to do a worse job than you could do for yourself?

She tried to keep her demanding full time job, an immaculate house, nurture a new baby and her husband, and it was simply exhausting. Everything began to unravel for her within the first few months.

She and her husband ended up quitting their jobs and moving closer to family. They are both doing well now, but when I think of all the needless pain they went through because she was unwilling to accept "mediocre" help, I'm saddened.

## Delegating of the Job

Although situations vary with each job, there are areas that can be delegated to others. Schoolteachers sometimes give extra credit to students who volunteer to help clean up the classroom. This is a wonderful way to delegate.

But some work situations don't easily lend themselves to delegation. For example, take the case of the secretary who regularly washes the office dishes, coffee mugs and picks up the half-and-half…without compensation. Depending on the corporate culture, she may be able to negotiate a little extra time off and/or pay for herself if she can't get out of doing these things.

Here's how…by keeping a running log of exactly how much time she spends performing these duties that are not germane to the job!

If the time is substantial, an employer might decide that it's better for the company's bottom line to provide paper cups, utensils and creamer. Or a supervisor may post a sign to remind everyone that "Your mother doesn't work here, if you use it, wash it, dry it, and put it away! —The Management" (Yes, I have seen this note posted in an office kitchen.)

A subtler—but equally effective—idea is for the company to order a personalized coffee mug for each employee for in-office use only. From thereafter, it'll be obvious who left their cup out.

In a career situation where the workload is unbearable, it's necessary to find out *exactly* what is eating up so much on-the-clock time. When you determine this, you are in a position to find a solution or alternative that would benefit the company and/or your supervisor.

It's imperative that you answer the WIIFM question. As soon as you approach your supervisor, though keep in mind, the same question will be running through his or her mind. For your own sake, tell them what's in it for *them* quickly. It should be the first thing out of your mouth.

Whenever you start a request for change by answering that WIIFM question, you are much more likely to get what you want. People make changes because there's something in it for *them*.

My five-year old son already knows this well. When he wants something, he has learned to approach me with the benefits that *I* will receive.

"Mommy, if you let me have one piece of candy
from my goodie bag, I promise I'll eat all my dinner.

One piece of candy for me right now will give you a nice happy dinner."

"I don't know sweetheart, you've got to practice writing your name when we get home, and I'm concerned that the sugar will make it hard for you to sit still and concentrate."

"No it won't, Mom. I'll be so happy you gave me my candy that I'll go straight to the table and do my work. You won't have a hard time about homework...if you let me eat my candy."

Under the cross-examination from the master litigator, I begin to waffle. After all, a willingness to do homework and a happy dinner are hard to resist.

"Are you sure you won't spoil your appetite and you'll do your homework...with no hard time?"

"Positive, Mommy," he says, already sensing victory.

"Okay, Daniel. One piece. Please don't make me regret this."

"I won't, Mom. You're the best mother in the whole world!" he says emphatically, thus smoothing over my lingering doubts with his lavish praise.

Notice how he never once talked about how badly *he* wanted or needed the candy. Could I see that he was really motivated by his own benefit? Of course I could. Was I motivated to comply with his request anyway? You bet!

If you believe your current workload should be split between two people, or if you need an assistant or want to work from home, think long and hard about what's in it for *everyone else* if your request is granted. Write it down. Refine it. Show it to your mentors. Then tell your supervisor that you'd like to meet to talk about an idea that you've been working on to increase productivity.

I can't emphasize this enough. *Don't go to a supervisor with a problem without offering a potential solution!* A problem with no workable solution for the company is called a complaint...and managers/supervisors don't generally respond well to complaints—or complainers.

> *A complaint from a person reputed to be a complainer will seldom change anything. You won't get what you want by complaining.*

A complaint from a person reputed to be a complainer will seldom change anything. You won't get what you want by complaining.

Keep in mind that you may be able to do any one task better than anyone else on your job. You may be able to manage the house better than your husband ever could. You can probably fold laundry straighter than the kids, and you likely can put away your dishes better than any housekeeper.

But Superwoman does not exist. When you try to impersonate her, you aren't fooling anyone. Accept the help you can get, and be grateful for it.

## Prayer

*Lord,*

*There is so much to be done, and so few people to help me do it. Help the rest of the family see the needs and respond. I don't want to be an exacting taskmaster.*

Help me to delegate some of my responsibilities in a loving manner. Make those whom I ask receive these tasks with an open heart and a willing spirit. Give me the courage to risk being temporarily unpopular with the kids as I introduce and enforce these requirements.

Losing control over the details of maintaining our home is frightening to me. Help me not to over-react or give up when things don't meet my expectations.

You are in control, Lord. Enable me to rest safely in the knowledge that You are always with us, and that You love my family more than I possibly could. Help me to trust You even more, Lord.

*Amen*

Faith in Action ▶

List the top three things you could delegate to members of your family.

_____

_____

_____

_____

_____

Will you need to train them? Set a date and time to show them how to do it.

_____

_____

_____

_____

List the tasks at work that you can delegate.

_____

_____

_____

_____

_____

_____

# Multitasking

*"She sets about her work vigorously; her arms are strong for her tasks. She sees that her trading is profitable, and her lamp does not go out at night"* (Proverbs 31:17-18 NIV).

O nly one place in the whole Bible uses the plural form of the word "task." This verse refers to a woman who has children, a husband, a job in real estate, another job selling garments and a busy household to run. She's a working mother! Even though Proverbs 31 mentions that this working mother also has servants, God knows that with so much on her plate, she still has multiple tasks to accomplish.

In His infinite wisdom, God has left us the "Basic-Instructions-Before-Leaving-Earth" Manual (an acrostic for B.I.B.L.E.), giving us markers of the way in which we should go. In our times we call this ability to accomplish more than one thing at the same time "multitasking."

Successful implementation of this skill will free up time, make you more productive and reduce stress. Overall, it will be more enjoyable to get through a busy day.

Perhaps this is an appropriate place to point out that I have included stories from other working moms because my own wisdom and knowledge would barely fill up a pamphlet, let alone a book. Such was the case with multitasking. I admit, even I had to be convinced at first. Now I wouldn't have it any other way.

## Lessons from the Master Multitasker

Celia is a woman who is naturally very efficient. She's organized, dependable and even punctual. Almost nothing rattles her. Do you recall the typical morning scenario? The one with no meat taken out of the freezer for dinner, a sink full of dishes and the husband down to his last pair of clean underwear?

I proposed the following challenge to my friend Celia.

"What would you do when you came home on a night like that?" I asked.

After a moment's pause she responded: "I would sit the kids at the table and give them a light snack. Next, I would go downstairs and put a load of laundry into the washing machine."

At this point in her answer I rudely chose to interrupt her with the following excuse.

"Oh Celia, my kids wouldn't eat dinner if I gave them a snack so close to dinner time, and I could always do the laundry after they're asleep."

Undaunted, Celia continued with the following admonition. "Never forget that in front of the washing machine is an excellent place to cry and pray, Sabrina. If you give the kids something light to snack on, they won't be starving and irritable. While you're putting clothes in the washing machine, you can pray and think about what to do next."

"Then no matter what you decide to do," she added, "you'll be solving the dirty clothes problem at the same time. You could wash clothes, wash the dishes, cook dinner and get the kids started on homework all at the same time!"

> *In order to be effective, it is a reality that on occasion you are going to have to do two or three things at once.*

The expression "I can only do one thing at a time" simply does not apply to mothers who work both inside and outside of the home.

In order to be effective, it is a reality that on occasion you are going to have to do two or three things at once.

Ever since your first child was a minute old you have had to multitask. Think about the standard labor-and-delivery scenario of feeding the baby while you smile for the camera and answer the doctor's questions!

## Freeing Up Time = Freeing Up Space

Imagine a child's set of wooden stackable blocks. If your child is anything like mine, they go through a stage where they line them all up end-to-end, creating a long straight train. This is wonderful, except that it takes up far too much room so, as dutiful moms, we all pretty much insist that when they are done, they stack them up somewhere. (This conserves floor space.)

The blocks can't be stacked too high or they will fall. They must be stacked low enough not to fall over, but high enough to open up floor space. A balanced ratio between the two is needed.

Try to think of multitasking as stacking your activities one on top of another so you can free up your time. In Celia's scenario, by giving the kids a snack, starting laundry, praying, then tackling the dishes and dinner, she stacked five tasks in a one-hour time period. The beautiful thing is that we can all learn to think and prioritize like this…especially in the midst of less-than-ideal circumstances.

## What's in It for You?

The benefits of stacking activities together (or multitasking) are:

1. You will increase your productivity.
2. You will increase your amount of free time.
3. You will conserve your energy.

*The idea is to try to make a game out of finding ways to multitask.*

From the time you wake up in the morning until you go back to bed at night, try to think of things in your usual routine that can be multitasked.

For example, you can even multitask some activities while

you're asleep! Start with a coffeemaker that has a built-in timer and set it for the time you wake up. This is a powerful incentive to get out of bed for some people.

Even if you forget to set it the night before, you can still multitask coffee-making with shower-taking—two tasks at once. While waiting for the water to warm up, you can brush your teeth—three tasks at once. You could even shave with "Nair" hair remover—now you are up to four tasks…simultaneously.

The idea is to try to make a game out of finding ways to multitask.

## First Things First…with Good Reason!

A word of warning, I strongly urge you to begin perfecting this skill *after* you have implemented the previous three secrets into your usual routine.

First, ask for God's guidance in prayer; second, pare down your commitments and unproductive time wasters; and third, delegate appropriately. After you have implemented these you are ready to perfect the art of multitasking.

If you try to multitask before the other areas of your life are in place, you will end up being more productive at doing things you shouldn't be doing in the first place! It would be like taking the expressway towards burnout instead of the scenic route.

> *If you try to multitask before the other areas of your life are in place, you will end up being more productive at doing things you shouldn't be doing in the first place!*

## Your Commute

Getting back and forth to work each day represents a significant block of time for some people. Many people try to use the time in their car, train or bus to unwind. After all, there's not much else to do while fighting traffic.

Actually, there can be a way to unwind and multi-task at the same time. Start by listen to inspirational music (classical is my personal favorite) or listening to audio books. Bibles are available on CD and cassette. It's a great way to listen to what God has to say. Maybe you could use a hands-free cellular phone to keep in touch with your relatives and friends.

If you take the bus or train, you could read a book, write letters, or use a laptop to get the jump on your workday. Or you could just sleep. And yes, technically speaking, sleeping during your commute can be considered multitasking. You are doing two tasks at once—getting to work and getting some rest!

In a nutshell, these are your first four secrets to phenomenal success.

First, ask God to give you wisdom (and mentors.)

Second, eliminate extraneous activities.

Third, delegate appropriately.

Fourth, multitask the things that you—and only you—can do.

It is an eye-opener to think about how much time is actually saved, and how much more productive you can be when you multitask instead of single-task. Multitasking is your ticket to having more time and increased productivity. For a busy working mom, having more of those two precious commodities is an answer to prayer.

## Prayer

Lord,

You are a marvelous, gracious, loving God. I'm so grateful that You take an interest in even the smallest details of my life. I want to do only what You consider to be the best for my family and me. I ask You to bless me with amazing direction and productivity. Give me the energy to accomplish those things that are in harmony with Your will.

Bless me with a cheerful attitude. Keep me ever mindful that showing love for my family and spending time with them comes before checking off activities on my to-do list.

Somehow, Lord, make me productive, loving, patient, and joyful...all at the same time. You are the God of all possibilities, and I ask for this miracle with the trusting faith of a child.

*Amen*

## Faith in Action

List three things you can multitask regularly in the morning.

_____

_____

_____

_____

List three things you can multitask regularly in the evening.

_____

_____

_____

_____

What can you do to make your commute more productive?

_____

_____

_____

_____

_____

_____

# Show Up...
# Big Time

*"Dear friend, take my advice; it will add years
to your life. I'm writing out clear directions to
Wisdom Way, I'm drawing a map to Righteous
Road. I don't want you ending up in blind
alleys or wasting time making wrong turns"*
(Proverbs 4:9-11 The Message).

Consider this secret to be the unwritten rule of the
workplace.

It's likely no one you trust has ever pulled you aside
to clue you in on exactly how to be a great employee and
a great mom. The majority of working moms learn the
unwritten rules of succeeding in the workplace and at
home the hard way...by making a lot of mistakes.

Childless women in the workplace don't usually
know these secret rules exist, and they don't always
apply to working dads. The trouble is that experienced

working moms may be unsure if they can trust you enough to give you this warning.

Right now, think of me as an experienced working mom pulling you aside to give you some insider workplace advice.

Start by being aware that there are still widely-held stereotypes and prejudices against mothers in the workplace. These are just a few of the perceptions that you may find yourself up against:

a. She won't be able to handle the job.
b. She won't be committed to getting the job done right.
c. She can't be depended upon.
d. She'll quit the first chance she gets.
e. She doesn't want to be here.
f. She'll do the bare minimum required to keep her job.
g. Her family situation makes more work for everybody else.

In all honesty, the same things could be said about any employee, regardless of their family situation. But if you're a working mother who is absent from work, late getting there or has to leave early to take care of the kids, watch out!

Even if everybody else comes in late, calls in sick and goofs off, *it will stand out more when you do it.* Being a working mom who is guilty of taking the same types of liberties as "everyone else" is just like putting a target on your back. While it's possible no one will take aim at you, it sure makes you an easy mark.

And that isn't fair.

That isn't right.

It might not even be legal.

Somebody ought to do something!

True, somebody really ought to buck the system and change things. Without the hard-fought battles of women before us, few of us would even have a high school education. Someone truly does need to shake things up in the modern workplace. If you feel called to be that person, I (along with countless others) would be grateful.

But if directly fighting against those stereotypes and prejudices seems like more than you wish to tackle at this point in your life, here's the secret to helping you avoid them...and maybe even eliminate them in some small measure.

As we discussed, coming in late and calling in for one reason or another will make a small minority of people resent you. This can make trouble for you when it begins to escalate to verbal jabs or potshots taken at you behind your back or in your presence.

It usually begins with some form of bad-mouthing—little jokes or light-hearted remarks about your commitment and contribution in the workplace. Seemingly good-natured references to how you probably won't be able to do something because of your kids.

These do not always spell impending disaster, but they should be considered a red flag. Once you are in

> Remember, in the working world, it is always easier to maintain a good reputation than to rebuild one.

the position of having to "prove" yourself, it will consume time and energy that would be better spent doing your job, or being with your family.

Remember, in the working world, it is always easier to maintain a good reputation than to rebuild one.

### That's Already Happening—What Now?

Don't worry, here's the plan if you've suddenly realized that you have a minor (or major) drama unfolding. It's pretty easy to turn your reputation around and, in doing so, experience the flexibility to respond to the occasional child-related issues.

The first thing you will need to do is to be punctual. I can't emphasize enough how much better your quality of life at home and at work will be if you show up on time for work.

Establishing safe, reliable and enriching care for your child while you are at work is one of the greatest challenges you will face. Depending on the age of your children, this would be a baby-sitter, day-care center, grade school, an after-school program or a latchkey.

Setting up a Plan A, Plan B, Plan C and Plan D for childcare will significantly maximize your dependability as an employee.

"Plan A" is your usual working/childcare routine. "Plan B" is the routine you follow when your child is sick or school is closed, but work is not. "Plan C" is for when Plan B falls through. "Plan D" is the plan of last resort.

## Plan A

Most likely, you have already given some thought to setting up a Plan A scenario for childcare while you work. For toddlers and babies, this would be a baby-sitter or daycare center. For school age kids, this is a regular school day and before or after school programs. For the older child, this might include a latchkey.

If you are just starting out as a new mother or are unsatisfied with your current childcare situation, the following tips will make it easier to set up a routine that works well for your family.

Start with something that will work *right now*. Don't spend a lot of time worrying about what might be needed in another year or two. Meet your current needs as best as you can now.

> Why compromise on childcare that works for now in anticipation of what might be needed later?

Why compromise on childcare that works for now in anticipation of what might be needed later?

In the case of babies and toddlers, the more individualized, quality care you can provide, the better. These can include having a trusted relative baby-sit, a nanny, au pair or even working opposite shifts from your spouse.

The positives of having one-on-one care for your child are that your child will have a caregiver's undivided attention. Your child will be frequently held, attended to and nurtured. At this young age, you needn't be overly concerned about curriculum; their primary lesson to learn is that they are loved.

If the childcare is in your own home, this is another positive. Your mornings and evenings will run a whole lot smoother when you don't have to pack up your child, lunches and a diaper bag.

The negatives of having one-on-one care for your child are first, if your caregiver is sick or unable to care for your child, you'll need a ready replacement.

Having a one-on-one childcare provider can also be expensive. A live-in nanny or au pair can also intrude on your family life.

You also are placing a great deal of trust in this individual. Thus, it is vitally important that you check the background of anyone who will be left alone with your child.

Many means are available to obtain background information on the person you are considering hiring to care for your child. Our website, www.workingmom.com, can give you inexpensive background checks. The peace of mind you receive from this inquiry is invaluable.

Nanny-cams have also become popular in recent years. These are small surveillance cameras, which can be hidden throughout your home. If you are going to have one installed in your home, it's wise to inform potential applicants from the start.

As the saying goes, an ounce of prevention is worth a pound of cure. Your child's safety is more important than the risk of offending an applicant. It's also nice to know in advance if your childcare provider would object to your scrutiny.

Rather than have one-on-one in-home care, some families opt to utilize a family daycare. This can be a person who takes care of several children in her home during the day.

The positives are that this is a home-like setting. There may be only a few other children in the home. The caregiver is also very likely to have experience with children; she may be a mom or grandmother herself.

This type of care is also generally less expensive than a nanny or au pair.

The negatives are that if the caregiver is sick or unavailable, you may not have a ready replacement. Some family daycare providers are also not as rigidly regulated as professional daycare centers. Furthermore, installing a nanny-cam is usually out of the question...after all, it's not your house.

Next let's examine professional daycare centers, also known as preschools. (The term "preschool" carries less of a stigma to the outside world than the term "daycare.") When I told friends or relatives, "My children were accepted into a preschool near my office," I received a generally positive reaction. However, when I would say: "My children are in a daycare center next to my office," the reactions often were varying degrees of pity for my kids, along with contempt for me.

If you find yourself in the midst of a hostile-towards-working-moms-crowd, consider pulling out the following phrase: "Accepted into an Early Learning Program." You will probably still be labeled as pushing your kids too hard too fast...but at least it's a different label.

The positives of preschool are early and later dropoff, more options if the regular caregiver/teacher is sick and it typically includes an educational curriculum. Also, preschools are generally regulated to some extent by state or local government.

The negatives of preschool are the high turnover in staff, higher incidence of kids getting sick and a higher ratio of caregiver to child.

It is possible to utilize a combination of these methods in obtaining childcare. In fact, combining options is the ticket to being able to show up…big time at work. I'll give you an example of how our family does it.

We have a trusted relative come to our home to care for each baby until they are old enough to attend preschool. However, in case the caregiver is sick, on vacation or otherwise unavailable we have a Plan B. This is essential to reduce the number of days that my husband and I miss work.

## Plan B

Your "Plan B" for childcare is utilized when a child is sick or if schools are closed—but work is not. This quandary has the highest likelihood to affect work performance and employee attendance.

It doesn't have to cause major upheaval if you plan for the unexpected…in advance. In our case, I asked my prayer partners, mentors and trusted friends who stay at home if they would mind being one of several people I could call on if I found myself in a last minute scramble for childcare. I described the most likely scenario to be an unexpected snow day, or a mildly ill child.

Generally speaking, people are more willing to lend a helping hand on a "per diem" basis versus long-term. The advantage to setting up a pre-set course of action (other than you missing work) is that if you have spoken with people prior to the need arising, you don't have to feel as if you are calling "out of the blue" to ask for a favor. It's easier to ask for help if you have pre-qualified the potential request.

Many preschools allow you to register your child on a per diem basis—if space allows. Even if your child normally has one-on-one care, you will be grateful you took the time to proactively pre-register when your Plan A childcare falls through.

Start by checking with the newer preschools in your area. When they first open their doors, many schools are still building their enrollment, and are more likely to allow pre-registered children on an as-needed basis. Usually, all you have to do is fill out the application, pay the registration fee, the cost of the day's care and keep your child's immunization records up to date.

"Expect the unexpected."

Consider this to be the mantra of life as a working mother. Establish a plan to address the inevitable turn of events which will leave you in the lurch for childcare. This is not an "if" question, it is a "when" question.

Even a first-time mother in the workplace can anticipate this. What separates the women from the girls is whether or not you have a proactive plan to respond— other than you calling in saying you can't make it to work. The primary benefit to having Plan B in place is that it will put an end to the desperate mad dash which occurs when a child can't go to school.

## Plan C

There will be times, however, when only *you* will do. If your child is more than mildly ill, or if your Plan B falls through, either you or your spouse will have to take time off work to care for the child. We have all had to do it. The way to go about it will vary, depending on your company's policy—both written and unwritten—on sick-child time.

Let me encourage you to do the following: try to minimize the use of sick days for yourself whenever humanly possible. This serves a twofold purpose.

If you have a reputation for never missing a day's work, you will develop a reputation for being diligent. This serves you well during those times that you need to call in.

> If you have a reputation for never missing a day's work, you will develop a reputation for being diligent. This serves you well during those times that you need to call in.

Remember, no one at work wants your germs any more than you want theirs. And don't halfway kill yourself by working when you need to take the time to heal. You'll only make things worse.

You will have to prayerfully consider how much information you give when you call in sick to care for a child. As a general rule, less is more. Women tend to offer more explanations for their actions than men, and you could end up talking yourself into saying something you don't want to say. If you're unsure of what to say, here are some standard answers you can personalize to suit your style.

"I won't be coming in today."

"I'm going to take a sick day today."

"I'll need to use a personal day today."

Did you notice that all three examples are statements? No questions. No *asking* permission to be sick. You're a grown woman, not a kid in the principal's office. By all means, resist the urge to ramble. No lengthy diatribes about the well-being of your family.

Speak to your supervisor, not one of your co-workers or your boss's secretary. If you have to leave a message, try to do it on a voicemail, rather than have someone else take a message.

When you speak to a human being, they may ask you if something is wrong or if everything is okay. This is where I urge you to remember the "less is more" principle.

Scenario: You've been up all night with a kid who has a 103° fever. You don't think you should go to work.

Response: "Thanks for asking. I'll be fine. I've been up all night with a fever and I'm in no shape to come into work."

Tell the truth. Always. But try to avoid placing the blame for your absences on your child. It may come back to bite you in some form or another.

## Plan D

Plan D is the plan of last resort. This is when you've gone through everyone on your Plan B list, you simply cannot call in sick and your child can't go to school.

If your child is not sick, and school just happens to be closed, you might consider bringing him or her to work with you. In this case, bring something to play with that has the potential to hold a great deal of attention. I'm not usually an advocate of pocket-sized electronic games, but this would be a good time for one.

Some local hospitals have "sick child" programs available. Call your area hospitals *in advance*, to check. Then pre-register, even if you seriously doubt you'll ever use it. An ounce of prevention is worth a pound of cure.

Lastly, you might allow an older child to stay home alone. This is an individual call on your part. At a minimum, your child should be responsible enough to adhere to some basic safety rules:

No using the stove.

No visitors.

Only answer the phone if it's me. (If you don't have Caller ID, then have a pre-arranged ring.)

No Internet.

No going outside.

What you should do in an emergency.

What *is* an emergency?

As a rule of thumb, my own mother did not allow my brother and me to stay at home alone until we were pretty old—nearly in high school. And I'll confess, the first time was a little scary.

Again, Plan D should really be the plan of last resort.

When all is said and done, remember, putting a plan in place (especially a plan which includes a response to occasional catastrophes) will dispel most of the anguish involved with scrambling for quality childcare.

## Make a Big-time Impression

Now that you can show up for work, it's time to learn how to do it "Big Time." The Bible teaches us to be humble, but it also warns against false humility: "Let no one cheat you of your reward, taking delight in false humility" (Colossians 2:18).

If you have done a good job, you might think that it should speak for itself. Maybe it will, but maybe it won't.

And if you are working in the midst of a situation where there's someone just waiting to pounce on one false move of yours, it's foolhardy to think that performance alone will maintain your stellar reputation.

> If you have done a good job, you might think that it should speak for itself. Maybe it will, but maybe it won't.

This is yet another lesson I ended up learning the hard way. You simply must not fall into the trap of false humility—particularly if you are a working mother.

Every job has what are considered "star performers." You need to make a cold hard assessment about what activities and characteristics are most often praised about people on your job. Following your job description is a good start, but it's frequently not the only thing your performance is assessed by.

In some places, it's the number of voicemails you send out, or whether you send out e-mail with the time recorded late in the evening or early in the morning. Believe me, in some offices, these things do get noticed.

Something as simple as walking at a fast pace can enhance the impression of super-productivity. Some offices gauge an employee by sales, bringing in new clients or how many classes she teaches. It will vary widely, even within the same industry. This is why it is vital that you pay attention when a colleague receives praise. If you listen carefully to what is said about the star performers, you'll have most of the information you need to make a big-time impression of your own.

## It's Working! What Now?

Learn to accept a compliment graciously. Practice this. I'm serious. Begin listening to how you respond to an accolade. Do you find yourself uttering statements that are falsely humble?

"Oh, it was nothing."

"Stop, you're embarrassing me."

"Whatever!"

This takes your big-time success and shrinks it down in an instant. It serves no purpose, because it's usually discomfort with praise and recognition that drives a woman to minimize her "moment."

*Another added benefit to having a third party's praise is that it holds a great deal of credibility and can be generally viewed as impartial.*

You have God's permission to let someone else praise you. "Let another praise you, and not your own mouth; someone else and not your own lips" (Proverbs 27:2).

Did you notice how the verse starts with "Let"? Let means "allow," "permit," and "do not prohibit." So eradicate the negative, downplaying tendency to respond without grace to a compliment.

For example, when you hear, "Great job on that project!", respond with something affirming and direct:

- "Thank you, I worked hard on it, and I'm glad you noticed."
- "That's nice to hear, thank you for telling me."
- "Thanks. Do you mind if I ask what you liked most about the project?"

This is definitely letting another praise you, and not your own lips.

Another added benefit to having a third party's praise is that it holds a great deal of credibility and can be generally viewed as impartial.

Think about it. Isn't it hard to believe the tales of a braggart when they go on and on about the feats they have accomplished? People seldom compliment people who have a reputation for "tooting their own horn." Maybe it's because everyone else has already heard their horn blow so many times!

You won't be a braggart if you do what Jesus commanded: "Let your light so shine before men that they may see your good works and glorify your Father in heaven" (Matthew 5:16).

## Prayer

*Lord,*

*Let me shine for Your glory, not my own. Use me to spread Your love, mercy and grace, even while I'm at work.*

You've given me such a tremendous love for my child. I'm certain that no one on earth loves my kid like I do. It's so very hard to entrust someone else to take care of this precious gift while I'm at work.

I ask you, Lord of heaven and earth, to personally watch, guard, comfort and reassure us while we're apart.

Put a hedge of protection around my child so that no harm in body, mind or spirit will ever befall. Enable me to make wise decisions in finding quality childcare, and in keeping up with the never-ending demands that are upon me at work.

I know I can't do this without Your guidance. I thank You for being my ever-present help.

Amen.

## Faith in Action

List the names of at least three people you can ask to serve as your Plan B.

_____

_____

_____

_____

_____

_____

Write out your new responses to compliments. Start with the two words "Thank you."

_____

_____

_____

_____

_____

_____

_____

_____

_____

_____

# Define Success

*"A good name is more desirable than great riches; to be esteemed is better than silver or gold"* (Proverbs 2:1 NIV).

The alarm clock finally went off. Chris looked at the time and turned it off. She really didn't need its help to wake up this morning. She had been tossing, turning and checking the clock all night long. This was going to be the day that would shape her whole professional career. Absolutely everything was on the line.

She got up and made herself a cup of tea, then she sat down at the kitchen counter with the new book her friend gave her. A Bible.

"I'll give it a try," she thought.

After reading (and not absorbing much) she put her head down and prayed.

"God, I really need You with me today."

She felt the presence of the Lord speaking softly to her. "I'm always with you."

"Yeah, well, I mean I *really* need You with me today."

Getting ready, she thought about how she had started with nothing, built a company of her own, made it hugely profitable and then entered into a partnership agreement with the three men she would face at today's meeting.

One of these men had recently begun to relegate her to the most menial tasks of running her division of the company, and had also begun speaking with open disrespect to her and about

> By the time she got in her car, she had a clear vision of Jesus with her.

her. The other two appeared to be falling in step with the ringleader. But Chris was nobody's chump. They would find this out today.

As she selected the right "power suit" for the meeting, an idea began to take shape in her mind.

If Jesus was going to be there with her, maybe she could imagine Him walking in with her, sitting in one of the chairs and being on her side.

She continued getting dressed with new vigor as she spoke aloud to Jesus.

"All right Jesus, if You're going to be there with me, what are You going to wear? You can't go in there with sandals and a robe. We've both got to dress right for this."

She occupied her mind (in her imagination), selecting a dark gray pinstripe suit for Jesus. She decided His hair would be one of the ponytails the young men of today were wearing.

By the time she got in her car, she had a clear vision of Jesus with her.

This is a wonderful example of calming the storms in life by keeping your eyes, heart and mind on the Lord. Know who's really in charge of everything and who holds the future.

So how did the meeting go? I'll tell you candidly; it appeared to have gone badly. It lasted from nine in the morning until after five in the evening, and she didn't even get up to take a bathroom break.

At one point, she was reduced to tears when she pointed out all she had sacrificed for the company. After all, these three men went home at the end of the day to their families, and she had never married, wasn't even dating anyone and could hear her "biological clock" pounding instead of ticking. Now her professional life was being turned into something terrible.

The ringleader became incensed! He went on a verbal tirade screaming and swearing at her with the foulest curses he could think of. He had never done this to her before in plain sight of the other two partners.

In that instant, it became clear that this partnership could not work. In the end, Chris ended up mortgaging her house and taking out a loan to buy back her stake in the company. She re-started it with just one friend who was willing to work for next to nothing initially to get it going again.

Incidentally, the Lord also worked out the problem with her pounding biological clock. She fell in love with and married a long-time friend and they had a little girl.

"Trust in the Lord...and lean not on your own understanding" (Proverbs 3:5).

From Chris's story you can learn that when you take the power of the Lord with you, He will work all things together for good for those whom He has called according to His purpose (see Romans 8:28).

> *This doesn't mean that everything that happens is good. It isn't. But there's the promise of good to come.*

This doesn't mean that everything that happens is good. It isn't. But there's the promise of good to come.

Think about organic fertilizer—which is really a fancy name for cow manure. It would seem that there is absolutely nothing good that can come out of cow manure. It smells bad, it's messy and there's usually a lot of it in what would otherwise be a beautiful pasture.

But God works even that into something good. Doesn't fertilizer (when used right) make the pasture even more beautiful? Give God the worst situations in your life, and ask Him to make something beautiful out of them.

Change requires effort. Sometimes, the effort seems so great that remaining in the same situation appears to be the most viable option. But remember this (and you can quote me), "The life you are leading is real. This is not a dress rehearsal."

## Go Fly a Kite, or Two, or Three

Have you ever flown a kite? You need a good amount of wind (but not too much). You need a long string (but not too long). You need a big kite (but not too big). And you need time and patience.

It's kind of hard to fly a kite...if you ask me. Now try to imagine flying two kites at once. This would seem theoretically possible if you started one first, had that up in the air and then got the next one airborne. It would be difficult to do it alone, but under the right set of circumstances, it could be done.

Now try to imagine getting three kites to fly at once by yourself. Nearly impossible, you might conclude. Not worth the effort.

As a working mom, you already have two kites in the air—your family and your job. They are both up in the air on a long string, and it's all you can do to keep the wind from tangling them together. If the winds of life come on too strong, you'll end up with your "kites" falling down or blowing away.

> If God has put these types of longings in your heart, He will make a way for them. But the time of transition for any type of change can be tough.

Adding a third kite would seem ridiculous. Why would anyone want to do that when they can barely manage what they have now? Because maybe, with God's help, you could be flying the two kites that *He* wants you to fly.

Perhaps something in your family's structure needs to change. Maybe there's a better way to manage your career. Or if you finished your education, maybe more options might be available to you. Perhaps you're being called to start a whole new career!

If God has put these types of longings in your heart, He will make a way for them. But the time of transition for any type of change can be tough.

Like the old expression says, "A bird in the hand is worth two in the bush." And there's wisdom in the refrain, "Don't quit your day job." (This is especially valid when you need that job to put food on the table.) But don't let temporary discomfort stop you from achieving your destiny.

Through it all, you have God to help you through the toughest transitions. Victory is when preparation meets opportunity.

Megan sacrificed a great deal to attain her professional and personal goals. Her story is inspiring, especially to me, because I'm not certain I would have had her steely determination to persevere. She had justifiable reasons to get sidetracked and, in the short run, it would have been easier for her. But she stayed the course, and here's her story.

While finishing her last year of nursing school, Megan and her husband discovered she was pregnant. The baby would be due around spring break. She was excited about motherhood, but how could she finish the last few months of school with a newborn? How could she study for final exams? What if she went into labor earlier than expected? What if it were later?

Some people advised her to quit school and go back and finish when the baby was older, but she did the opposite. She buckled down, studied hard and had her baby over spring break. She had only ten days before classes started again, but she finished, graduating with a Bachelor of Science in Nursing.

She then went on to get a job with good pay as a nurse in the hospital's cardiac unit, and that's when she noticed the pharmaceutical reps coming in and out of the hospital. She wondered if being a pharmaceutical representative would provide a better quality of life.

I'll let her tell you in her own words.

"Megan, you're a registered nurse. Why did you decide to leave the nursing field?" I asked.

"I realized that I had reached a plateau in my career. There was really no more opportunity for advancement. Aside from the patients, the reward for hard work wasn't there and there was no recognition for it. Even if I was the best nurse on the floor, there wasn't any recognition for the achievement."

"Was recognition important to you?"

"It was and still is. I even initially took a pay cut to come into pharmaceutical sales, but I knew in the long run, there would be more opportunity. With the raises, bonuses and compensation package, I could make far more money."

"Do you think that having your four-year degree played a role in getting the job you wanted?"

"Well, sure. It opens up opportunities," she replied.

"Tell me about your first interview with a pharmaceutical company."

"Before I went in, I saw it was a predominately male environment, but I knew I had a lot to offer. I made sure that I didn't disclose anything that could even be perceived as a weakness."

"Like what?"

"Well, I certainly didn't go in there and say, 'By the way, I'm going through a divorce, and I have a kid that I'm raising on my own!'

(*Laughs*)

"I kind of read the vibes during the interview, and went along the same direction. This guy saw an ambitious young nurse who was up for a challenging change of career. I just went with it."

"What happened next?"

"I could tell he really liked me throughout the interview. I got the job."

"But your story doesn't end there. How did you tell your company that you had a child?"

"I waited until I had already started initial training, then I asked my boss how I could apply for health insurance for my son. I could tell he was completely floored to find out that I had a child."

"What did you do for childcare?"

"I had a lot of help from my mom, and I was used to working long hard hours so I knew it really wouldn't be a problem. You know, I only had a ten-day maternity leave when I had my son. It was one of the hardest things I've done in my life," she answered gravely.

"Getting back to childcare, I understand you've remarried and have a new baby. What did you end up doing for childcare this time?"

"The baby goes to a lady's house from our church. The last of her kids went off to school and she's been a stay-at-home mother her whole life."

After being hired, Megan immediately went on to become one of the top representatives at the company...her *first* year...the *next* year...and the year after that!

She was right. She did have a lot to offer.

She also had plenty of justifiable reasons to sidetrack her long-range goals. If she hadn't suffered through her last few months of school, what kind of position would she have been in to support herself and baby when her first marriage ended?

Nursing paid well and had flexible hours. She could have justifiably continued that career path. But she would never have been able to get the recognition she thrives on today. She also wouldn't have gotten the company car, bonuses and awards earned by top representatives.

Because she is not in an traditional office setting during working hours, she is free to respond to any child-related situations without having to secure a backup (as she would in the nursing field). Furthermore, if she needs to call in, it's not announced to her co-workers as it doesn't concern them.

## Aim for What You Really Want

"If you aim at nothing, you'll hit it dead center every time." –Ben Hawkins (My dad)

The key to Secret 6 is to create goals that will enable you to be the best you can be. This applies to your life both personally and professionally.

By now, you can probably guess the first thing to do before you set your goals. *Pray.* And ask your prayer partners to pray for you. Also ask your mentors to tell you what they think your strongest attributes are.

When you pray first, you can be clear about the direction God is leading you. And when you seek the counsel of other godly women, you will gain perspective and direction on how to best live it out.

> *When you pray first, you can be clear about the direction God is leading you. And when you seek the counsel of other godly women, you will gain perspective and direction on how to best live it out.*

You may already have a dream, wish or vision for what you would like your life to be. Dreams, wishes and vision are important, but never confuse them with a goal. Wishes are stagnant. You can wish, dream and visualize until the cows come home without making a single stride towards actualizing what you want.

Many people fall prey to staying too long in the wishing, dreaming and imagining phase of fulfilling their God-given destiny. It is far more purposeful if you start by seeking for God's leading in your life. After all, He designed you, and He has much greater perspective and clearer vision for your destiny.

To set your goals, make them specific and measurable, and then clearly outline the steps to take to quantify your progress.

For example, a mother of very young children might start with the following declaration: "I will spend more quality time with the family." This is a nice wish. Even if she can imagine clearly what she would do with this quality time, it is still not a goal...until it gets more specific.

"Spend one hour a day, five days per week reading or coloring with the children." This is a clear image of what she wants to do. There is even a measurable time frame included, but it still doesn't qualify as a goal. It's really just wishful thinking until you include the steps to actually make it actually happen.

"Starting today, spend the hour between dinner and bedtime reading or coloring with the children instead of washing dishes. Dishes will be washed after the children are already in bed."

Bingo! That's a goal.

Remember this expression: "When you have no idea where you're going, you're guaranteed to get there." You don't have to end up going nowhere personally or professionally when you plan ahead and set your goals.

Redefine Success.

Plan for it.

Work towards it.

## Prayer

*Lord,*

*I pray that You would bless me with ears to hear the sound of opportunity knocking. I ask that You would give me the courage to open the door, and the stamina to walk through...even when it's difficult.*

*It's my heart's desire to be successful at home and at work. Let me define success not by the world's standards,* nor those of my friends, relatives or strangers on the street, but by Your standards. I'm looking to follow Your perfect plan for me. Help me to know what that is.

I confess that it's been hard for me to know Your will, let alone live according to it. So many voices compete for my time, telling me to turn away from Your plan. Sometimes I feel powerless to make a decision to follow You, Lord.

It's been said that if I'll take the first step, You'll take the second, third and fourth steps, and when I look back on my journey, I'll realize it was You who took the first step too!

Let it be so with setting new goals for my future. Bless me with a constant sense of Your presence, Lord. I thank you and I praise You with all of my heart, mind and strength.

*Amen.*

## Faith in Action

What was the first thing that came to mind regarding setting a goal for your professional life?

_____

_____

_____

_____

What was the first thing that came to mind regarding setting a goal for your personal life?

_____

_____

_____

_____

What will you need realistically to accomplish these goals? (For example, additional education for your professional life, or setting up a savings account.)

_____

_____

_____

_____

_____

_____

# Replenish
Your Spirit

*"Are you tired? Worn out? Burned out on religion? Come to me. Get away with me and you'll recover your life. I'll show you how to take a real rest"* (Matthew 11:28 The Message).

S abrina, your idea for a book sounds great. Just make sure you put something in it about how to get enough sleep. That's what I want to know." This question has been posed to me over and over again.

Last year, during my reign as Mrs. New Jersey in the Mrs. America Pageant, I selected encouraging working moms as a platform. I never imagined how big of a platform it would prove to be. There are so many different areas that need encouragement.

So far, we've discussed the secret to: creating a support system, paring down time wasters, delegating, multitasking, showing up for work and setting goals.

There's now just one thing left to cover. It is the overwhelming, all-encompassing, mind-numbing fatigue in body, mind and spirit that working moms live with.

## Sleep

There's a very good reason why you are so tired—simply put, you don't get enough sleep. How much do *you* actually get each night? If you crawl into bed around 11:00 and watch the evening news until 11:30, what kind of shape are you going to be in when the alarm clock goes off just a few hours later?

> You need to rest even more than everybody else… because you've got more to do when you're awake!

Even if you fall asleep within a half hour of turning in, when your alarm goes off at 6:00 A.M. you've only slept for six hours. That's 25 percent less sleep than most doctors recommend! If you only net out six hours of sleep per night, then you start your day only three quarters rejuvenated. (No wonder people drink so much coffee these days!)

Just being somebody's mother is a full-time job. Now add to that a home to keep up, plus a job in the paid workforce. The last person on earth to deliberately start out behind the eight ball should be a working mom.

You need to rest even more than everybody else…because you've got more to do when you're awake!

It may sound obvious, but I'll tell you anyway: Get sufficient sleep by going to bed earlier! Don't tell yourself that watching TV at night helps you unwind. Television will keep you awake until you literally crash. If you really need to unwind, reading would help you do it better than the news or a sitcom.

Here's a little tip about reading at night. I have this "thing" about finishing what I start. For me, it's supremely difficult to put down a good book that I haven't finished yet. Reading at night has the potential to keep someone like me awake until three in the morning in a quest to find out how the book ends. That isn't wise when there's work the next day. But there is a solution.

I discovered (quite by accident) that collections of short stories work well at night. You can start and finish an entire story in the span of five to ten minutes, and then put the book down with a sense of accomplishment. Take a look at www.workingmom.com for some of my favorite short story collections.

## See Your Doctor

I'm not a doctor or a nurse, but let me advise you to see one as there's always the possibility that your tiredness could be exacerbated by an underlying medical condition, most of which can be easily remedied.

For example, when I was a teenager, my parents noticed that I slept a lot. Initially, they thought it was because I was staying up too late at night talking on the phone. They also assumed that it was just a part of being a teenager. Both assumptions were correct. But after one particularly difficult morning, my mother declared that she was going to have me checked out by the doctor if I was *that* tired.

She made good on the threat, and took me in to see the pediatrician. I was already sixteen years old, and felt embarrassed to have my mother in the office explaining how hard it was to wake me up in the morning.

The pediatrician checked me out, and ran a series of blood tests. When the results came in, she called my mother. "Your daughter is very anemic. She needs to start taking iron supplements right away. I'm also going to try to figure out what's causing her anemia."

## The Trait

The pediatrician got together with my parents' doctors and checked their medical histories. They found that my mother had the trait for sickle cell anemia. This trait is a harmless condition that some people are born with. It makes them less likely to catch malaria, but more likely to be low on iron in their bloodstream (also known as being anemic). Not enough iron in the bloodstream would make anyone tired. If I had inherited the trait, this would explain my anemia. The doctor called my mother and asked her to bring me in for another test.

The results for this test came back that I *did* have the trait for sickle cell, like my mother. This explained the fatigue. The doctor said that if I would take an iron supplement or multivitamin with iron regularly, I wouldn't be so tired.

*If you're always tired, save yourself the aggravation of imagination and go see your doctor for a yearly physical.*

We never would have figured out how to regain my energy if my parents hadn't taken me to the doctor. We could have blamed the phone or my adolescent hormones. Maybe someone could have said that I was depressed, or had chronic fatigue syndrome, or a thyroid problem or Lyme disease. There are a host of conditions that can cause fatigue.

If you're always tired, save yourself the aggravation of imagination and go see your doctor for a yearly physical.

## Nutrition and Health

Have you ever seen a kid with a heavy bookbag strapped onto her back? Some must weigh nearly twenty pounds. It makes me tired just to look at them carrying such a heavy burden. It must be exhausting.

It's time to get personal. If you've got twenty pounds or more to lose, then it's making you tired. Everywhere you go, you have the equivalent of a heavy backpack or burden on you.

I'm not telling you anything you probably haven't already figured out for yourself. But, I've been there. In fact, after the birth of my second child (the one I stayed on bed rest for) I tipped the scale at a whopping 200 pounds...okay, if I took off my watch, jewelry, hairclip, clothes and exhaled, I was 199.5 pounds.

I'm not over six feet tall, so it didn't look good on me. In the weeks that followed the birth of my child, I slimmed down to 167 pounds, and sort of leveled off at a size 16. But I could squeeze into a 12 if it was cut "right"—and squeeze is exactly what I did.

It was these scenarios that inadvertently led to my participation in the Mrs. America pageant. And it isn't what you might think.

## How It Really Happened

I was at a sales training meeting, and during a break, I mentioned to some colleagues that I was thinking about writing a book for working moms. They said it sounded like a great idea. At the end of the conversation, I made the joke, "Bet you if I was Mrs. America my book would just fly off the shelves!" We all laughed and I thought that was the end of it.

It wasn't.

Have you ever been made to feel like a fool? That's exactly what happened to yours truly when one of the ladies from the break said to the rest of our group, "Sabrina, why don't you tell everyone about your idea?"

Naturally, I thought she was talking about the book and I started going over some of my ideas. She interrupted me with the smuggest look I've ever seen on the face of a human being. "Not your book...tell them about your plan to be in the Mrs. America Pageant."

Now, believe me when I say that you had to be there. This was not a simple misunderstanding. It was meant to make fun of me. You see, at that point in my life, I had my hair in dreadlocks, had never plucked my eyebrows and I definitely needed to lose some weight.

The rest of the group began to chime in, "You can do it! Why not? You're attractive!" They were all just being polite. I could tell they were all thinking, "She's not bad-looking, but I can't believe she thinks she's a beauty queen!" The more I protested, the more they felt obligated to tell me to go for it.

I called my husband during the next break in tears. This is rare for me, because I'm not one to cry often. I told him the whole story and how I wanted to quit my job because I couldn't face everyone.

In one of those moments where a husband says the right thing, Dan came out with this:

"You know, if a guy didn't like you, he would just say so. But women...women can be *evil!* But she picked the wrong woman this time...because you're the prettiest girl I've ever seen in my whole life."

"Well, you just think I'm pretty because I'm your wife," I whimpered (ever so slightly placated by his compliment).

"I'll tell you what we're going to do. We'll go over to your parents' house, log onto the Internet and find out what you have to do to be Mrs. America."

Thus began my foray into the arena of modern-day pageantry. My company, Pfizer Inc., sponsored me with Media Training and introduced me to the press.

Lenox China, the best fine china in the world, is made in New Jersey. They sponsored me by providing gifts to give to the contestants in the pageant.

Bernstein's, the place where I bought my prom dress over ten years before, sponsored me with gowns and interview suits.

Ellen Lange Skin Science sponsored me with weekly facials and microderm abrasion treatments.

My dentist office, Dental Plus, took out all my gray amalgam fillings and replaced them with white ones and whitened my teeth. (You should see me when I laugh with my mouth open...fabulous!)

The pressure was on, and I knew I had to quickly get in shape. I had seven months to lose 42 pounds.

Incidentally, even though there's no weight restriction on the Mrs. New Jersey or Mrs. America Pageant, I didn't intend to get up there out of shape.

Here's how I lost the weight. It was, in some ways, ridiculously easy. I kept eating everything that I normally eat, but simply stopped eating sweets, excessive pasta, rice, bread and chips. I filled up on salads, lean meats, seafood and and I drank water instead of sodas and juices. I ate strawberries sweetened with Splenda for snacks. My weight poured off.

> And the best part of losing the weight and increasing my muscle mass was the phenomenal physical energy! You won't believe how much pep you can put in your step when you're in good shape.

Now let me say this. I recommend that you speak to your doctor or a dietician before you implement any new diet or exercise plan. Just because something worked for me doesn't necessarily mean that it's right for you.

And I'll tell you the truth: The first three days of giving up the sweets and high starch foods were almost unbearable. Everywhere I looked there was a donut shop or bakery. After I made it past the third day, the cravings went away.

There's another thing you should know… A skinny girl can have a protruding tummy and arms and legs that jiggle. I know, because it happened to me and it looks as unsightly as it sounds. With the help of some trainers at the gym, I toned up within just a few short months by lifting weights.

And the best part of losing the weight and increasing my muscle mass was the phenomenal physical energy! You won't believe how much pep you can put in your step when you're in good shape.

Because of a working mom's time constraints, there are unique challenges to diet and exercise. Most of us don't have the time for traditional exercise programs, nor can we always eat balanced, nutritious meals. But if

> *The best part of losing the weight and increasing my muscle mass was the phenomenal physical energy!*

you watch the sugars and starches, if you make a commitment to work out with weights for a half hour, five days a week until you hit your goal, victory can be yours.

Incidentally, after you achieve your fitness goal, maintenance is much, much easier. I find that I can have the occasional sweet treat, and I now only need to work out once or twice a week.

When you employ reality-based approaches, victory is assured. The keys to reducing exhaustion are getting sufficient sleep, maintaining the right diet and increasing muscle tone.

## Spirit

Now that you know everything I know about replenishing the body, let's discuss the Spirit. There's no better place to go than to the Bible.

There are empowering, encouraging verses both in the Old and New Testament. The Bible has a great deal of encouragement for women and for employees, and examples of women who did both. There is value in being able to find and know what God says about each situation. For recommendations on Bibles I have found to be user friendly, check out the web site: www.workingmom.com.

The Bible has answers to even your most nagging questions. For example:

Worried about work? Deuteronomy 8:18 says, "And you shall remember the Lord your God, for it is He who gives you the power to get wealth."—NKJV

Worried about the direction your child is heading? Proverbs 22:6 says, "Train up a child in the way he should go and when he is old he will not depart from it."—NKJV

Other verses which speak to specific situations are:

Discouragement—Galatians 6:9
Family problems—Proverbs 29:15,17
Being a mom—Psalm 128:1-4
Worrying—Matthew 6:31-34
Dealing with criticism—Nehemiah 4:1-3
Conquering anxieties—Psalm 94:19
Loneliness—John 14:16-18
Discovering God's will—Isaiah 42:16
Forgiveness—Matthew 6:12
Processing anger—James 1:19
Growing spiritually—Philippians 1:6,9-11
Living joyfully—Psalm 100
Freedom—Romans 8:1-5
To be sure you're loved—Romans 8:38-39

I urge you to take the time to look up these Scripture references for yourself. Spend some time reading what God says about your life, your family, your job and you.

In case you haven't heard this before, God loves you. Really, truly, without reservation, loves you. He's always there, just a prayer away—even for the working mom.

## Prayer

*Lord,*

*Renew me. Replenish my body, mind and spirit. Enable me to soar. Make my heart and countenance light.*

*Lift my countenance when I'm discouraged. Strengthen my body when I'm tired. Give me the resolve to feed my body with healthy, life-sustaining foods. Lord, bless me with a dislike for those foods which do not bring health.*

*Above all else, surround me with the sense of Your presence. Give me a thirst for You, Your Word and Your people. Keep me forever in the center of Your will.*

*Amen.*

Faith in Action ▶

What are the top changes that you want to make as a result of reading this book?

_____

_____

_____

_____

_____

Who can you speak to for help in becoming the woman you desire to be?

_____

_____

_____

_____

_____

When would be the best time for you to read and study your Bible? Make a commitment to set aside time each day to replenish your spirit.

_____

_____

_____

_____

# Epilogue
## The New Typical Morning

*"Look at the nations and watch—and be*
*utterly amazed. For I am going to do something*
*in your days that you would not believe, even if*
*you were told"* (Habakkuk 1:5).

6:15 A.M.— Alarm clock rings.

6:16 A.M.— You smell the coffee brewing from the
kitchen. It's time to get up.

6:20 A.M.— Sitting at the kitchen table with a Bible
and a morning devotional book, you pray
for your family. You pray for your friends,
and that your work and the kid's school
will be edifying.

6:40 A.M.— Into the bathroom you go, multitasking—
shaving while the shower warms up while
you brush teeth.

7:00 A.M.— Makeup is on, hair is done, you are
dressed and ready.

7:05 A.M.— You gently wake up the kids. With a rub
on the back and a soft song, you open the

shades. You declare with sincerity "Rise and shine! It's a beautiful day and you don't want to miss it!"

7:15 A.M.— The children get dressed in the clothing they selected and laid out the night before.

7:30 A.M.— The family has breakfast together. Thanks to the microwave, you can make bacon, egg and cheese sandwiches in less than three minutes.

7:45 A.M.— You give them lunch money instead of packing lunch.

7:48 A.M.— You permit them to play with their toys after they have cleared the breakfast dishes from the table.

7:49 A.M.— You run the mental checklist...
   • Any field trips or permission slips needed today?
   • School fundraisers?
   • Is it show and tell day?
   • Library books?

7:53 A.M.— Wash the breakfast dishes.

7:58 A.M.— Take meat out of the freezer to thaw for dinner.

8:00 A.M.— The kids put on jackets and caps and wait for the bus. You pray with them for their upcoming day.

8:03 A.M.— Bus arrives.

8:05 A.M.— You calculate everything you'll need for work.

8:10 A.M.— While driving to work, you call one of your prayer partners using your "hands-free" cell phone from the car…just to check in and let her know you care.

8:20 A.M.— You arrive at work with ten minutes to spare. You quickly sit down at your desk and send e-mail and voicemail messages before 8:30.

8:29 A.M.— The boss walks in and finds you already hard at work. He comments, "I wish I had a dozen more employees like you!"

8:30 A.M.— You say "Thank you. I appreciate the compliment."

This promises to be an enriching day. This working mom has created a stellar reputation at work, and nothing is too hard to handle. Even if a child had been unable to go to school, there was a reliable contingency plan.

She has a personal relationship with God, and she has prayer partners. She has already eliminated extraneous commitments; she delegates appropriately and can multi-task the rest. She shows up, big time at work. She has her goals for success in sight, and is working towards them. She never lets her spirit run dry, because she regularly drinks from the wellspring of life through Jesus Christ.

What was once just a dream is now the typical morning.

## Prayer

Lord,

   Give me the resolve to follow You all the days of my life. Bless my family that they may follow after You, too. I'm onto something bigger than I can grasp. That's why I come before You asking You to hold onto me. I don't have the power to hold on to You.

   I love You, Lord Jesus. Thank You for saving me. I praise You, worship You and adore You. You are like no other person to ever walk the face of the earth. The whole world measures time by Your coming, and the years after Your arrival (B.C. and A.D.). Help me to remember that You are the Lord of everything, and even time itself is subject to Your authority.

   I ask that You hear my prayer in the name of my Lord and Savior Jesus Christ.

Amen.

## Faith in Action

Write your very own prayer here.

_____

_____

_____

_____

_____

_____

_____

_____

_____

_____

_____

_____

_____

_____

_____

_____

_____

# Appendices

# Pass It On!
# Be a Blessing

If you've been blessed by reading and working through this book, then you know firsthand what a difference a little encouragement can make.

Right now, there are probably several other working mothers you know who would benefit from learning the 7 Secrets to Phenomenal Success. The recommendation of a trusted friend is by far the most effective tool for changing the world in which we live. Your opinion carries more weight than any celebrity's with your friends, relatives and co-workers. Let them know if you feel this book is a tool that can help them. *Prayers for the Working Mom* was designed to be given to the people you care about.

We have created a special program for working moms who want to help others. When you call (212) PRAYERS and mention the "Be a Blessing" promotion, you'll save **30%** off the cover price for each book you order! Please call Working Mom Enterprises at (212) 772-9377 or (212) PRAYERS for more details on how easy it is to "Be a Blessing"!

You can change the world for working mothers, one book at a time!

# Spa Retreat?

Working Mom™ is launching a new series of weekend spa retreats. These retreats are designed to replenish your body and spirit. You can relax and be pampered for an entire weekend with other working moms like you. You'll receive a massage, facial, manicure, pedicure, and most importantly, time to reflect on your plans for success. You'll have all the time you need to pray and take a much-needed rest.

If you can't come to us, we can come to you! Why not schedule Working Mom™ to conduct a spa retreat near your hometown? Do you have a women's group, book club or nice group of friends that would enjoy a Working Mom™ Spa Retreat? We love getting to meet people personally, and our speakers/facilitators are among the best in the industry. You'll return home refreshed, with a focused plan for your future (and you'll look as good on the outside as you'll feel on the inside). It's an unforgettable weekend, one you'll always treasure. Contact us and find out for yourself how simple and affordable it is to have the experience of a lifetime. Our contact information is on the next page.

Working Mom Enterprises
Retreats
424 Park Avenue S.
Suite 200
New York, NY 10016

(212) 772-9377
(212) PRAYERS

Or you can log on to: www.workingmom.com to book us online. We hope to see you in person soon!

# Age Appropriate
# Household Job Chart*

### 3-4 YEAR OLDS CAN:
✓ Pick up toys
✓ Fold dishtowels and washcloths
✓ Match socks
✓ Put small items in the garbage
✓ Give food to pets
✓ Water indoor plants

### 5-6 YEAR OLDS CAN ALSO:
✓ Answer the telephone
✓ Sweep a deck/patio/porch
✓ Wipe the bathroom sink
✓ Put forks and spoons away
✓ Put their own clothes in the drawer
✓ Sort laundry into color piles
✓ Use a hand-held vacuum

### 7-9 YEAR OLDS CAN ALSO:
✓ Take out garbage
✓ Set the table
✓ Clear the table
✓ Vacuum an area rug
✓ Clean the inside of the car
✓ Empty the dishwasher

✓ Put away clean dry dishes
✓ Water the garden

## 10-12 YEAR OLDS CAN ALSO:

✓ Clean mirrors
✓ Clean kitchen counters and sink
✓ Fold and put away laundry
✓ Put away groceries
✓ Pack their own lunch
✓ Light yardwork
✓ Load the dishwasher

## 13-14 YEAR OLDS CAN ALSO:

✓ Clean the bathroom
✓ Change bed sheets
✓ Mow the lawn
✓ Wash dishes by hand
✓ Wash the car
✓ Do laundry
✓ Shovel snow

## 15 YEARS AND UP CAN ALSO:

✓ Use a leaf blower
✓ Use a snow blower
✓ Clean the refrigerator
✓ Reorganize storage areas
✓ Make dinner

* Ages listed are approximate and capabilities will vary depending on the individual child.

# Ultimate Grocery List

## STAPLES
Cereal . . . . . . . . . . . . ☐
Grits . . . . . . . . . . . . . ☐
Bread. . . . . . . . . . . . . ☐
Sugar. . . . . . . . . . . . . ☐
Buns . . . . . . . . . . . . . ☐

## CONDIMENTS
Ketchup . . . . . . . . . . ☐
Jelly . . . . . . . . . . . . . ☐
Peanut Butter . . . . . . ☐
Mayonnaise. . . . . . . . ☐
Olive Oil . . . . . . . . . . ☐
Salad Dressing . . . . . ☐

## PRODUCE
Apples . . . . . . . . . . . . ☐
Oranges. . . . . . . . . . . ☐
Bananas. . . . . . . . . . . ☐
Strawberries . . . . . . . ☐
Mangos . . . . . . . . . . . ☐
Lettuce . . . . . . . . . . . ☐
Celery . . . . . . . . . . . . ☐
Cucumbers . . . . . . . . ☐

## SPICES
Bacon Bits. . . . . . . . . ☐
Chocolate . . . . . . . . . ☐
Salt/Pepper. . . . . . . . ☐
Seasoning . . . . . . . . . ☐

## STARCH
Potato Mix . . . . . . . . ☐
Rice. . . . . . . . . . . . . . ☐
Spaghetti. . . . . . . . . . ☐
Sauce. . . . . . . . . . . . . ☐

## PAPER
Plates. . . . . . . . . . . . . ☐
Cups . . . . . . . . . . . . . ☐
Forks . . . . . . . . . . . . . ☐
Napkins. . . . . . . . . . . ☐
Paper Towels. . . . . . . ☐
Aluminum Foil . . . . . ☐
Toilet Paper. . . . . . . . ☐
Garbage Bags . . . . . . ☐
Zip Locks . . . . . . . . . ☐
Sandwich Bags . . . . . ☐

## PERSONAL

Soap . . . . . . . . . . . . . ❒
Shampoo . . . . . . . . . . ❒
Conditioner . . . . . . . . ❒
Detangler . . . . . . . . . ❒
Barrettes . . . . . . . . . . ❒
Lip Balm . . . . . . . . . . ❒
Skin Lotion . . . . . . . . ❒

## DRINKS

Apple . . . . . . . . . . . . . ❒
Diet Rite . . . . . . . . . . ❒
Juice Drink . . . . . . . . ❒
Water Filters . . . . . . . ❒
Coffee . . . . . . . . . . . . ❒
Decaf . . . . . . . . . . . . . ❒
Tea . . . . . . . . . . . . . . . ❒
Orange Juice . . . . . . . ❒

## FROZEN

Broccoli . . . . . . . . . . . ❒
Green Beans . . . . . . . ❒
Peas . . . . . . . . . . . . . . ❒
Corn . . . . . . . . . . . . . ❒
Mixed Veg . . . . . . . . . ❒
Ice Cream . . . . . . . . . ❒
Pizzas . . . . . . . . . . . . ❒
Fish Sticks . . . . . . . . . ❒
Nuggets . . . . . . . . . . . ❒

## CLEANING

Bleach . . . . . . . . . . . . ❒
Detergent . . . . . . . . . ❒
Dish Liquid . . . . . . . . ❒
Dishwasher Tabs . . . ❒
Fabric Softener . . . . . ❒
Light Bulbs . . . . . . . . ❒
Vacuum Bags . . . . . . ❒
Cleaning Wipes . . . . . ❒
Towels . . . . . . . . . . . . ❒
Windex . . . . . . . . . . . ❒
Bathroom Foam . . . . ❒

## CANNED

Olives . . . . . . . . . . . . ❒
Soups . . . . . . . . . . . . ❒
Red Beans . . . . . . . . . ❒
Black Beans . . . . . . . . ❒
Pink Beans . . . . . . . . ❒
Tuna . . . . . . . . . . . . . ❒

## DAIRY

Milk . . . . . . . . . . . . . ❒
Butter . . . . . . . . . . . . ❒
Cheeses . . . . . . . . . . . ❒
Eggs . . . . . . . . . . . . . . ❒
Creamer . . . . . . . . . . ❒
Yogurt . . . . . . . . . . . . ❒

## BABY

Diapers . . . . . . . . . . . ☐
Wipes . . . . . . . . . . . . ☐
Baby Food. . . . . . . . . ☐
Formula. . . . . . . . . . . ☐

## MEATS

Beef. . . . . . . . . . . . . . ☐
Chicken. . . . . . . . . . . ☐
Sausage . . . . . . . . . . . ☐
Bacon . . . . . . . . . . . . ☐
Turkey. . . . . . . . . . . . ☐
Fish . . . . . . . . . . . . . . ☐

## MISC

_____ . . . . ☐
_____ . . . . ☐
_____ . . . . ☐
_____ . . . . ☐
_____ . . . . ☐
_____ . . . . ☐

# Other Resources That Bless

24-Hour Telephone Ministries:
- 888 NEED HIM
- 800 NEW LIFE

Family Ministries:
- Family Life Today: 800 FL TODAY
- Focus on the Family: 800 A FAMILY

Calm the Kid-Commute/Stimulate the Imagination:
Audio Books:
- Adventures in Odyssey
- Chronicles of Narnia
- Lord of the Rings

Books to organize a Working Mom:
- Family Managers Guide for Working Moms, Kathy Peel, Ballantine
- Survival Guide for Busy Women, Emilie Barnes, Harvest House
- The Messie Manual, Sandra Felton, Revell

Websites:
- http://www.workingmom.com

Bibles:
- The Message Bible, Eugene Peterson, Navpress
- The Listeners Bible, Max McLean, NIV

# Acknowledgments

Daniel, You are the absolute love of my life.

Daniel, Christiana and Angelica, You are truly blessings.

Calvin and Benjamin Hawkins, Thank you bringing me into this world. I love you.

Whitney Malone, Thank you for always believing in me.

Christiana Foglio Palmer, You were right. This was a great idea.

Yvette Vega, What an example of a godly, praying woman.

Celia, Pete, Matt, Julie, Grace and Olga, Thanks for your prayers.

The Presbyterian Church in New Brunswick, Thank you for nurturing my faith.

Fawnya, Marcus, Darius and Saraya Gibson, Thank you-welcome.

The 4 Helens: Hubbard, Williams, Scudder and Byrd, You are true mentors on a mission.

Agatha Asamoah, Irene Buerle, Martha Decker, Eva Nagy, Leslie Bagley, Grace Farkas, Millie Skerbetz and Beth Scibenski, Everyone should have prayer partners like you.

Kelly and Jason Hawkins, I love you guys. You're like a brother and sister to me.

Tasha and Colleen, at Dr. Jorgenson's office, You were with me at the start.

Dr. Stark, Eiges, Rossi and staff, You treat me like an insider, and I'm grateful.

Dr. Geller, Nee, Marmora and staff.

Dr. Marino, Dr. Tulio, Brown, Catanese, and Cathy, Anne, Erin, Aliaz and staff.

Dr. Goldberg, Cernadas, Beim, Johnson, Karanikolas, Salley and LaBosco, Thank you.

Frances and Verleea McDonald, I love you more!

Thelma and Keith Pegram…and Joey, Thanks for all the love throughout the years.

Judy and Richard, We still keep you in our prayers.

Sonya and Arthur, Move closer to home!

Felicia, Man-man, Binky, Shannon, Julisa and Shardell, I love you.

Uncle Bro, I miss you. Your city is on the cover.

Larraine, Lynette, Mark, Cheyenne and Shanell, See you soon.

Kelly, Danny, Jake Robert, Finn and beautiful Elsa, I love you.

The Dickensons, I love you.

Diane, Greg, Heather, Cortney, Kayla and Gabi, We're proud to call you friends.

Claire Huttemeyer, What a voice. It's a gift.

Deb, Clint and Lauren Hall, What would we all do without "The Halls of Justice"?

Lynn and Jim Styczynski, Yes, yes, we know how to spell it!

Delia, Roger, Zayne, Quinn and Allana, I told you I'd put your name in the book.

Felicia, Dave and Hannah, Definitely, friends forever.

Debbie, Bob, Ryan and Taylor, You are the definition of a lifelong friend.

Sandy Jaffe, Thank you for always being a friend.

Word of Faith Baptist Church in Alabama, Keep doing His will.

Detective Ronald Hawkins, I still want a PBA card!

Jamielah, Larry, LeShaun, Ben, Madarius and Tyrone, I love you.

Camille, Terrence, Terra and Nick, It's been too long.

Deirdre, Jim, Ryan, Robert and Delaney, You're in our prayers.

Sam Tauton, You are inspiring!

Lisa Middleton, Thanks for taking a preview.

Keven Talbert, You're a born encourager.

Caroline Phipps, You're the kindest former MP I know, thanks for the encouragement.

Jack Currie, Thanks for the help with balance.

Walter Bowers, When I grow up, I want to be like you.

Mike Nachezel, Positive Mental Attitude is you all the way.

Allyson, You are an encourager.

Little Lauren, I bet you thought I'd forget…I didn't. Thank you.

Big Lauren, You've been a true friend to our family.

Faye, Lauren, Louise and Bill, You are part of what makes church a family.

Szabi Nagy, Pastor, deep theologian, editor and friend, thank you.

Karen, Amy, Amira, Allison, Janine, Sam and Lauren, You have extravagantly blessed us.

Roz Noonan, You can really, really write. You're a great
editor.

Chuck Dean at ACW Press, You made this book so much
better. Thank you.

Fred Renich at ACW Press, You are a blessing to authors
and readers alike.

Victor Hudson, God used you to encourage the comple-
tion of this book. Thanks.

Laurett Ellsworth Arenz, You are beautiful inside and out.
Thank you for being there.

Monica and John Thompson Jr., May God bless you for
blessing us.

John Reilly, You are a great boss.

Steve Sacchetti, You were a great boss too.

Clayton Young, You are a great boss's boss.

Carl Wilbanks, You were a great boss's boss too.

Karen Katen, You are a great boss's boss's boss's boss (and
no, I don't get to boss anyone, so don't bother to
look).

Rose, Mafalda, Alaina and Nolan at American Harvest,
Thanks.

Russ Bloss, (hey, Bloss rhymes with boss), You are the
absolute greatest.

Justin, I still have your autograph.

Linda, Katie, Patricia, Sean, Megan, Elizabeth and Chloe,
I love you.

Toni, Bill, Julian and William, You put the "A" in adven-
ture.

WAWZ, Star 99, I've grown so much with you, you're a
blessing.

Focus on the Family, You've taken me from milk to solid food.

Family Life Today, You were pivotal in helping reshape my family. God bless you!

Traci Wilson, Janet Olchowicz, Sue Gross and Anne Malone, You are great counterparts, friends and mentors.

Ginger Taylor, There's no one I'd rather have watching my back in a foxhole, thanks.

Linnea and Chuck Maloney, What would I have done without you? Thanks.

Mrs. America Pageant, Thank you for the experience of a lifetime.

Fran and Richard Krauss, You are absolute transformers with a camera and makeup.

Barnes & Noble, Thank you.

Borders, Thank you, and I love your coffee.

Target, You make it easier to be a busy mom. Thank you.

Wegmans, I never dreamed a grocery store could be such a blessing!

Wal-Mart, Everything I've ever wanted, you have, and you have it quickly. Thanks.

Christianbook.com, Thanks for keeping me up to date in my faith.

Faithworks, Where would we be without you? Thanks.

One Way Advertising, Thanks for making the World Wide Web less sticky.

To God, the Father, Son and Holy Spirit, I'm yours. Do with me what you will.

# *Prayers for the Working Mom*
# Order Form

**Postal orders:**  Working Mom Enterprises
424 Park Avenue S.
Suite 200
New York, NY 10016

**Telephone orders:** 212-772-9377

**E-mail orders:** orders@workingmom.com

**Please send *Prayers for the Working Mom* to:**

Name: _____

Address: _____

City: _____  State: _____

Zip: _____

Telephone: (_____) _____

## Book Price: $10.99

**Shipping:**  $3.00 for the first book and $1.00 for each additional book to
cover shipping and handling within US, Canada, and Mexico.
International orders add $6.00 for the first book and $2.00 for
each additional book.

or contact your local bookstore